palm-size SOFTIES

First published in the United States of America in 2010

Creative Publishing international, Inc., a member of

Quayside Publishing Group

400 First Avenue North

Suite 300

Minneapolis, MN 55401

1-800-328-3895

www.creativepub.com

Visit www.Craftside.Typepad.com for a behind-the-scenes peek at our crafty world!

**Creative Publishing
international**

Originally published in Japanese language by Boutique-Sha, Tokyo, Japan

Copyright © Boutique-Sha

English language translation & production by World Book Media, LLC info@worldbookmedia.com

ISBN-13: 978-1-58923-561-8

ISBN-10: 1-58923-561-4

10 9 8 7 6 5 4 3 2 1

Printed in China

contents

Gallery

Cheeky Chihuahuas

Designed and
handmade by
Miyoko Tachibana

Big personalities often come in small packages. These little guys are always up to something! If you let them out of your sight, things can get crazy.

These two have been sewn with light blue fleece and striped knit jersey.

SIZE:
4¾ inches
(12 cm) tall

Instructions
on page 45

1 Chihuahua (Marin)
2 Chihuahua (Sky)

3 Peanut
4 Coco

bandy dogs

Coco and Peanut take great offense when they're referred to as "hot dogs." Who can blame them? With soft fleece and colorful cordlane "coats," they are a dashing dachshund duo.

He doesn't have papers and he doesn't care! Max knows he's a good-looking mutt in beige corduroy.

SIZE:
4½ inches
(11.5 cm) tall

Instructions
on page 49

5 Mixed breed
(Max)

Mutts rule!

Jimmy Jack Russell and Billy Bull love to ruff house, but don't mistake that black eye for an injury, these breeds are known for their spots. With a cotton swab rubbed in pastels (see page 44), you can make a whole litter, each with different markings.

SIZE:
5 inches
(12.5 cm) tall

Instructions on page 49

7 Jack Russell terrier (Jimmy)

SIZE:
4¼ inches
(11 cm) tall

Instructions on page 49

6 Bull terrier (Billy)

designed and handmade by Miyoko Tachibana

Jimmy Jack Russell and Billy Bull Terrier

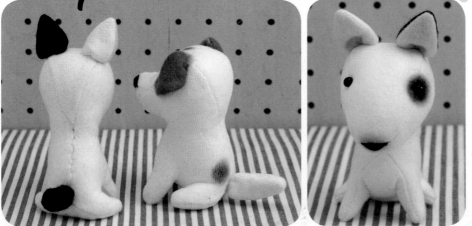

Feeling blue? Olga and Pedro will fix that. These pint-sized pugs will cheer you right up, so take them wherever you go!

SIZE:
4¼ inches
(11 cm) tall

Instructions
on page 49

8 Pug (Olga)
9 Pug (Pedro)

8

9

Olga & Pedro

Old Friends

designed and handmade by Akiko Kawana

Dudley and Arthur are country dogs who lead a quiet and peaceful life. Just give them a squeeze and your stress will melt away.

SIZE:
7½ inches
(19 cm) tall

Instructions
on page 52

10 Dog (Dudley)

10

With his head tilted to the side and those sweet eyes, Dudley will stick with you through thick and thin.

SIZE:
7 inches
(18 cm)

2 Instructions
on page 52

11 Dog (Arthur)

11

Is he is smiling or is he
asleep? Who's to say, but
he's cute as a button!

Charlie and Randy are ready for bed. Their footed pajamas are sewn from soft jersey, which is very cozy!

SIZE:
7½ inches
(19 cm) tall

Instructions
on page 54

13 Rabbit (Randy)

12

13

SIZE:
6¼ inches
(16 cm) tall

Instructions
on page 54

12 Monkey (Charlie)

Pocket Pets

designed and handmade by Akiko Kawana

SIZE:
6 inches
(15 cm) tall

Instructions
on page 56

14 White Bear (Snowy)

SIZE:
5¾ inches
(14.5 cm) tall

Instructions
on page 56

15 Kid (Cupcake)

14

15

Snowy and Cupcake are a stylish pair! Made out of terrycloth, they are ready for anything.

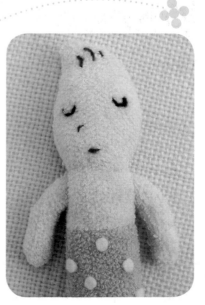

Teddy bear Picnic

designed and handmade by Mamiko Arakawa

These lanky bears always picnic in **style**.

16

17

SIZE:
9 inches
(22.5 cm) tall

Instructions
on page 57

16 Girl Bear (Paula)
17 Boy Bear (Howie)

Paula and Howie show off their country chic. Just look at her lace skirt and dotted apron and Howie's twine suspenders. How cool!

Never miss an opportunity to look your best!

Cats and Bears and Pandas, oh my!

designed and handmade by Harumi Satou

Each are made from the same pattern with just a few changes to their faces.

SIZE:
4 inches
(10 cm) tall

Instructions
on page 60

18 Panda (Huang Huang)
19 Bear (Henry)

SIZE:
4¼ inches
(10.5 cm) tall

Instructions
on page 60

20 Cat (Minou)

Tea time is their favorite time. Minou takes milk in her tea, while Henry and Huang Huang prefer honey in theirs.

Buttons are used to attach their arms and legs.

HENRY

HUANG
HUANG

MINOU

Wonky & Wonderful

Designed and handmade by Miyuki Toriu

Yes, we all waddle when we walk, but we don't let that get in our way! Toby is a cool dog with a derby hat and necktie, Gigi is a stylish cat with a beret, and Kate is a fashionable rabbit with a flower on her ear.

SIZE:
5¼ inches
(13.5 cm) tall

Instructions on page 62

21 Dog (Toby)

21

sweet

SIZE:
5 inches
(13 cm) tall

Instructions
on page 62

SIZE:
6 inches
(15 cm) tall

Instructions
on page 62

22 Cat (Gigi)

23 Rabbit (Kate)

Choose your
favorite printed
fabrics and give
them matching
tops!

22

23

Retro Pets and Pop Companions

Designed and handmade by Ayako Iwakami

Disco fever has come to town! Take us out clubbing with our hair piled high and our green eye shadow. We'll be your most fashionable accessories!

24

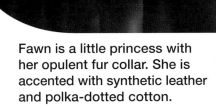

Fawn is a little princess with her opulent fur collar. She is accented with synthetic leather and polka-dotted cotton.

SIZE:
6 inches
(15.5 cm) tall

Instructions on page 65

24 Fawn

25 Pony

25

SIZE:
6 inches
(15.5 cm) tall

Instructions on page 65

Stylish Pony is as poised as a prince. He and Fawn are fast friends!

Bunny's fur is so soft you will want to rub her against your cheek, but don't let that fool you. She'll dance all night.

SIZE:
5¼ inches
(13.5 cm) tall

Instructions
on page 68

26 Bunny

Squirrel's pompadour and wide eyes make him look like a bad boy.

SIZE:
3¾ inches
(9.5 cm) tall

Instructions
on page 68

27 Squirrel

**29 Rabbit
(Zoe)**

**28 Bear
(Anders)**

A Storybook Romance

Designed and
handmade by
Ayako Takekawa

Pals, Anders, and Zoe are a great couple with their dog Kenken and Mimi the cat. Who says you can't live happily ever after?

Anders's and Zoe's arms and legs are easy to pose, so you can create more chapters in their story.

SIZE:
2¼ inches
(6 cm) tall

Instructions
on page 75

31 Cat (Mimi)

30

SIZE:
2½ inches
(6.5 cm) tall

Instructions
on page 75

30 Dog (Kenken)

31

Fight like cats and dogs?
No way, this cat and dog
are best friends.

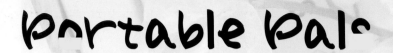

portable Pals

designed and handmade
by Ayako Takekawa

They're small enough to take anywhere. Attach your little
friends to a bag or cell phone, and you'll never be alone.

32

33

Bright colorful felts give
these petite pals extra
charm. Striped or
polka-dotted scarves
are a great accent.

SIZE:
2¾ inches
(7 cm) tall
....
Instructions
on page 77

SIZE:
3 inches
(8 cm) tall
....
Instructions
on page 77

33 Penguin (Palmer)

32 Monkey (Violet)

Betsy is lounging around, watching TV on
her rug. You gotta love vacation days!

SIZE:
2¼ inches
(6 cm) tall

3 Instructions
on page 79

34 Pig (Betsy)

Terrycloth favorites

designed and handmade by keiko Matsuda

Five terrycloth animals, each one sweeter than the last.

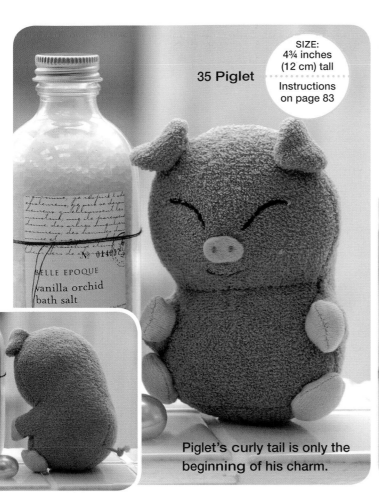

35 Piglet

SIZE:
4¾ inches
(12 cm) tall

Instructions
on page 83

38 Panda

SIZE:
4¾ inches
(12 cm) tall

Instructions
on page 84

Piglet's curly tail is only the
beginning of his charm.

Everyone loves Baby Panda's
fetching black-ringed eyes.

SIZE:
4¾ inches
(12 cm) tall

Instructions
on page 83

36 Seal

SIZE:
5 inches
(12.5 cm) long

Instructions
on page 81

37 Hamster

SIZE:
5 inches
(12.5 cm) long

Instructions
on page 84

39 Frog

Seal's little round body
is ready for hugging.

Hamster greets the world with
a mischievous smile.

Frog's wide mouth always makes us
laugh (or maybe give him a kiss?).

Kiki is a fun girl, stylish from her hat to her boots. She is often seen in the company of her hip boyfriend, Nick.

One Doll, Many Characters

designed and handmade by Kayo Suzuki

Hana and Kiki are best friends. They like dressing up when they go out.

Nick and Hana meet on the way to Kiki's house. Such taste! Their conversation is uproarious.

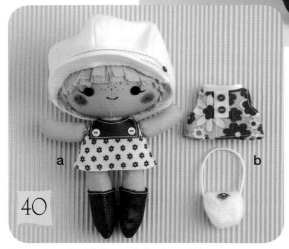

40

a

b

Instructions for Kiki's wardrobe (a and b) on pages 88–89

Instructions for the bag collection on pages 89, 91

41

a

b

Instructions for Hana's wardrobe (a and b) on pages 90–91

42

a

b

Instructions for Nick's wardrobe (a and b) on pages 92–94

SIZE:
5 inches
(13 cm) tall

Instructions
on page 85

40 Girl (Kiki)
41 Girl (Hana)
42 Boy (Nick)

Cutie Kid Dresses Up

designed and handmade by Ayako Iwakami

Cutie is a fashion doll with big charming eyes. She takes her inspiration from the 1970s and loves matching her hats and bags.

43

Cutie goes on a date

SIZE:
5 inches
(13 cm) tall

Instructions on page 95

43–45 More Cuties

Cutie is ready for her date!

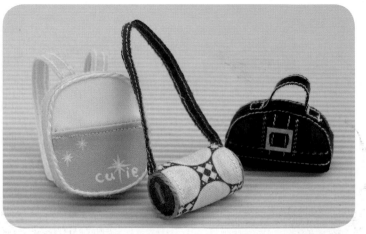

Instructions for making the clothes and accessories on pages 98–103

A hairband with goggles to hold back
Cutie's hair? How go-go!

Tall boots and plaid
are the height of
Brit-pop style. Her
checkered hat and
red hair complete
the picture.

These little animals, decorated with flowers, bring happiness wherever they go. Keep them with you, attached to your cell phone or bag for luck.

Pippi the duck has a tail made from pom-poms. It may not be anatomically correct, but it sure is cute. Give her a soft touch by using a combination of wool and felt.

SIZE:
4 inches (10.5 cm) wide

Instructions on page 104

46 Duck (Pippi)

Lucky Pals

Designed and handmade by Junko Francesca

SIZE:
3 inches (8 cm) tall

Instructions on page 107

48 Toy Poodle (Dandie)

What is this kitty dreaming about? Her eyelashes are decorated with sweet beads.

47

SIZE:
4 inches
(10 cm) wide

Instructions
on page 105

47 Cat (Lily)

48

Happiness exudes from this pink toy poodle. Place Dandie in a small box and give him to someone special.

Even bears wear diapers sometimes. Make these funny triplets with a soft pastel felt.

49

50

51

Baby Bear Triplets

designed and handmade by Kayo Suzuki

SIZE:
3½ inches
(9 cm) tall

Instructions
on page 108

49–51 Bear Triplets

These baby bears, with their pink cheeks and silly eyebrows, make wonderful gifts for a shower.

52 He-Goat
53 She-Goat

Goat Groupies

designed and handmade
by Keiko Matuda

These goats with their plump bodies and skinny legs are giving their hoofs a rest after a lot of dancing!

The original goatee!

52

53

The heart-shaped accents on their tummies show that these goats aren't fooling around. They are serious fans!

Prairie Bunny

designed and handmade by Emi Ozaki

This bunny is all country with her tweed and gingham. Her arms are attached to her body with buttons and can move up and down.

54

SIZE:
5 inches
(13 cm) tall

Instructions
on page 110

54 Prairie Bunny

Bunny puts on her lace bonnet and flowered apron before going square dancing.

Her bag is accented with an appliqué apple.

Good Night Bear

designed and handmade by Emi Ozaki

Good Night Bear is made from the same pattern as Prairie Bunny. Stitch his eyes closed so he can go to sleep.

SIZE:
4¼ inches (11 cm) tall

Instructions on page 110

55 Good Night Bear

Good Night Bear has his pillow with him … but he feels so sleepy … Can he make it to his room?

55

… Oh no! He fell asleep before he got there!

ZZZ

TOOLS

Scissors
Small sharp scissors work best.

Craft glue
It dries transparently.

Fabric marker
Water-soluble fabric pen marks are easily removed with water.

Tracing or tissue paper
Use to trace the sewing pattern onto tracing paper.

Pins

Soft sculpture (doll making) needles
Use a long needle to attach eyes and nose.

Embroidery needle
These sharp needles glide easily through fabric.

Awl
Use to make small holes.

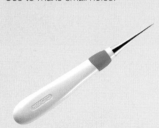

Pliers
Use to pull needles out of tight fabric and also to tighten cotter pins.

Mallet
Use the stick end for stuffing small areas.

Cotter pin tool
Use to turn cotter pin when attaching arms and legs.

Buttons
Use for the eyes and nose to create lively facial expressions.

Stuffing
You can change the firmness of body parts by adjusting the amount of stuffing.

Pastels
Use to draw features such as cheeks and freckles.

Pellets
Plastic granular material useful for adding weight.

Embroidery floss
(unless noted in the book, use six-strand embroidery floss)
Use to embellish nose, eyes, arms, legs, etc.

(A) Six-strand embroidery floss (it's common to use one or two strands to sew)

(B) Pearl cotton (single-strand embroidery floss, size 5 or 3)

Buttonhole twist thread
A strong thread that won't easily break; use to attach eyes and nose.

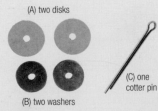

Joint set (5 pieces)
Use to attach arms and legs.

(A) two disks

(B) two washers

(C) one cotter pin

OTHER TOOLS:
Construction paper
(for pattern)

TECHNIQUES

How to Transfer a Full-Size Pattern

① Place tissue paper onto pattern and trace

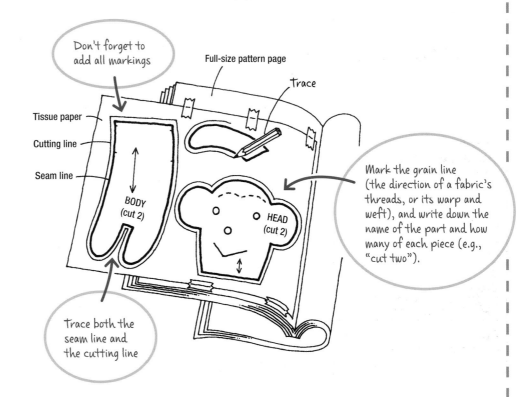

Don't forget to add all markings

Full-size pattern page

Trace

Tissue paper

Cutting line

Seam line

BODY (cut 2)

HEAD (cut 2)

Mark the grain line (the direction of a fabric's threads, or its warp and weft), and write down the name of the part and how many of each piece (e.g., "cut two").

Trace both the seam line and the cutting line

How to Transfer a Pattern Without a Seam Allowance

① Cut out the tissue paper pattern. Place it on top of the thicker paper, and carefully trace around the shape (this will be the seam line).

② Cut out the pattern on thick paper on the cutting line.

③ Trace the pattern onto the wrong side of the fabric. Draw a consistent seam allowance on all sides of the pattern (either ¼ inch [6 mm] or ⅝ inch [16 mm]); this is the cutting line.

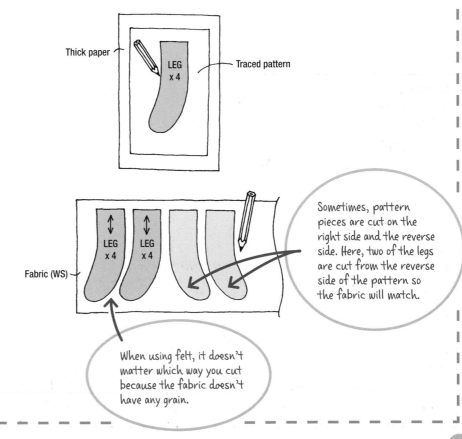

Thick paper

LEG x 4

Traced pattern

LEG x 4

LEG x 4

Fabric (WS)

Sometimes, pattern pieces are cut on the right side and the reverse side. Here, two of the legs are cut from the reverse side of the pattern so the fabric will match.

When using felt, it doesn't matter which way you cut because the fabric doesn't have any grain.

Transferring Patterns with Seam Allowances

① Place a tissue pattern on the wrong side of fabric, pinning it to fabric, and cutting them both out.

TIP

• When cutting two corresponding pieces, cut one with the pattern reverse-side up. This will produce, e.g., a left side and a right side.

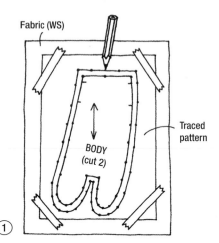

Fabric (WS)

Traced pattern

BODY (cut 2)

①

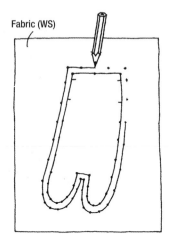

Fabric (WS)

How to Sew Two Pieces of Fabric Together

① Place pins perpendicular to seam line.

② Clip seam allowances for curve.

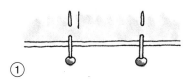

①

Basting (sewing with large stitches to hold the fabric in place) is usually not necessary but can sometimes be helpful.

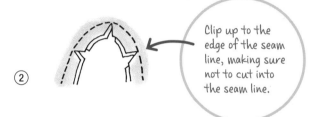

②

Clip up to the edge of the seam line, making sure not to cut into the seam line.

Basic Sewing Techniques

KEY

Right Side = RS

Wrong Side = WS

Whip stitch

Place fabrics together, and insert needle perpendicular to fabric. For two pieces of fabric on top of each other.

To attach a loop of string, pass needle between the two sides of the loop as shown in the picture.

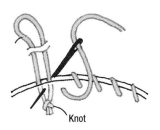

Knot

How to Attach an Ear

Attach the ear with craft glue, and then whip-stitch to head.

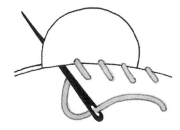

Ladder stitch

When the thread is pulled tight, only a small stitch will be visible.

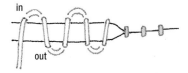

in

out

Vertical stitch

Like the whip stitch, the needle is inserted perpendicular to the fabric. For two pieces of fabric side by side.

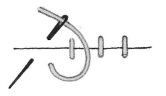

Back stitch

This is a secure stitch and good alternative to machine stitching.

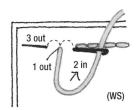

3 out

1 out   2 in

(WS)

How to Fill with Stuffing

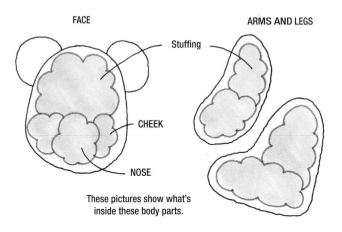

FACE

Stuffing

CHEEK

NOSE

ARMS AND LEGS

These pictures show what's inside these body parts.

How to Attach Eyes and Nose

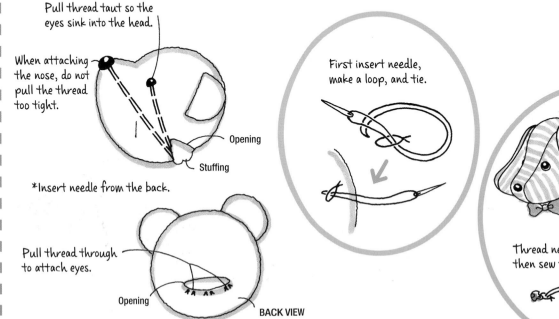

Pull thread taut so the eyes sink into the head.

When attaching the nose, do not pull the thread too tight.

Opening

Stuffing

*Insert needle from the back.

Pull thread through to attach eyes.

Opening

BACK VIEW

Thread type is 30th cotton thread.

First insert needle, make a loop, and tie.

HOW TO ATTACH RIGHT AND LEFT EYES TOGETHER

Thread needle through button, then sew through face as shown.

How to Attach the Head, Arms, and Legs

HOW TO ATTACH THE HEAD

The opening for stuffing creates an indentation that works nicely as a neck. This is also where the thread attaching the eyes and nose is pulled tight.

Join body parts using a whip stitch, ladder stitch, or vertical stitch. Try to take small stitches.

HOW TO ATTACH INFLEXIBLE ARMS AND LEGS

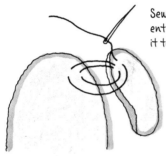

Sew through the entire limb to attach it to the body.

HOW TO ATTACH MOVABLE ARMS AND LEGS

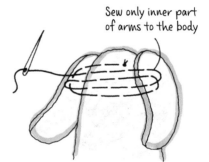

Sew only inner part of arms to the body

HOW TO ATTACH THE ARMS AND LEGS

Insert needle in the seam, and make a knot.

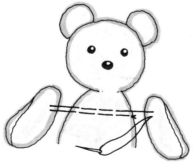

Attach a limb by sewing these 10 steps.

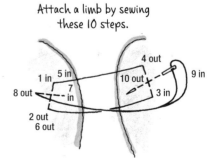

How to Create Facial Expressions

Create different facial expressions by changing the position of the doll's eyes and nose.

CHILDISH EXPRESSION

Place eyes and nose close to one another.

GROWN-UP EXPRESSION

Place eyes and nose farther apart.

FUNNY EXPRESSION

Place eyes and nose closer to the center of the face.

Creating Additional Features with Pastels

Use pastels or makeup such as rouge.

① Rub pastels vigorously across a piece of paper.

② Use a cotton swab to draw on spots or freckles.

Pastels

①

②

Cotton swab

Instructions for 1 Marin and 2 Sky, page 6

MATERIALS (FOR ONE)

- 15¾ × 6 inches (40 × 15 cm), Fabric A (1 cotton jersey, 2 fleece)
  6 × 4 inches (15 × 10 cm), Fabric B (1 fleece, 2 cotton jersey)
- Two 11-mm buttons for eyes
- One 8-mm button for nose
- 12 inches (30 cm) 7-mm satin ribbon
- Stuffing

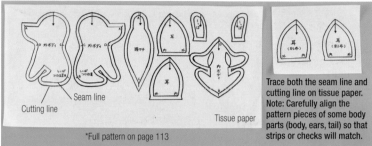

Cutting line

Seam line

Tissue paper

*Full pattern on page 113

Trace both the seam line and cutting line on tissue paper. Note: Carefully align the pattern pieces of some body parts (body, ears, tail) so that strips or checks will match.

MATERIALS

Fabric A (cotton jersey)

Fabric B (fleece)

Buttons

Satin ribbon

Stuffing

Thread (for eyes, nose, and stitching animal closed)

Sewing machine thread

*Contrasting thread is used in the instructions for good visibility.

TOOLS

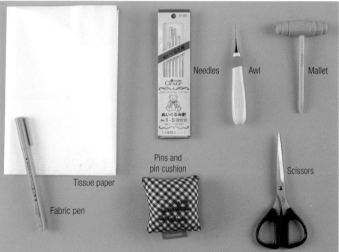

Needles

Awl

Mallet

Pins and pin cushion

Scissors

Tissue paper

Fabric pen

---

1 | Tracing and Cutting

① Place pattern piece on the wrong side of fabric B, mark dots every ¾ inch (2 cm), and pierce each dot with pen.

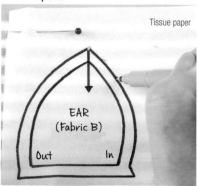

Tissue paper

EAR (Fabric B)

Out   In

② Remove the pattern and connect all the dots. Do the same for Fabric A.

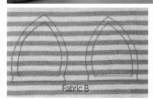

Fabric B

③ Cut the pattern piece along the seam line.

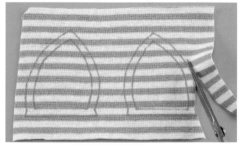

Fabric A

2 | Make the Body For stability, back-stitch at the beginning and end of all machine stitching.

① Pin Outer Body pieces together with right sides facing, from A to D.

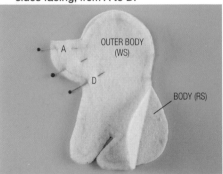

② Sew from A to D. Be sure to back-stitch at the beginning and end.

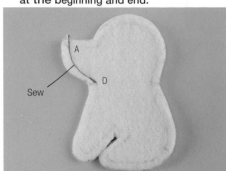

③ Pin one Outer Body and one side of Head Gusset together from points A to C.

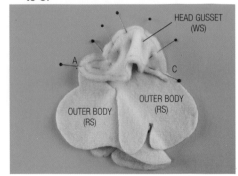

④ Sew from A to C.

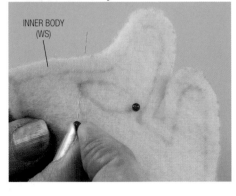

⑤ Repeat steps 3 and 4 for the second Outer Body and the other side of the Head Gusset.

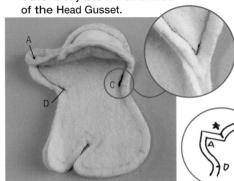

⑥ Clip the seam allowance to C, being careful not to cut into the seam.

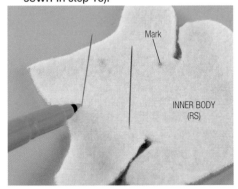

⑦ Place a pin on the edge of dart on wrong side of Inner Body.

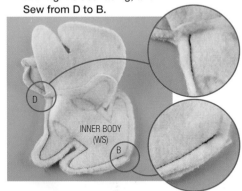

⑧ Mark the point on right side (darts will be sewn in step 18).

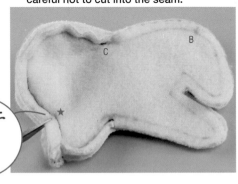

⑨ Pin Outer Body and Inner Body together with right sides facing, and Sew from D to B.

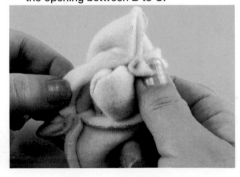

⑩ Repeat step 9 for other side of Outer Body and Inner Body.

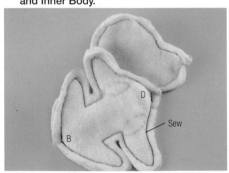

⑪ Clip to two points of the seam allowance, being careful not to cut into the seam.

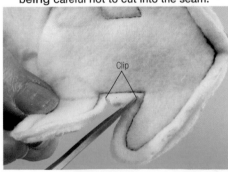

⑫ Turn body right side out through the opening between B to C.

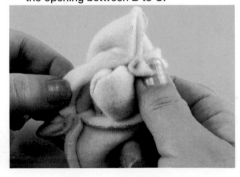

⑬ Use the awl to pull out small areas, being careful not to make a hole in the fabric.

⑭ Fill with stuffing (do not overfill).

⑮ Use the mallet (or a chopstick) to distribute stuffing evenly.

⑯ Take care when adding stuffing, as it is difficult to remold the body later.

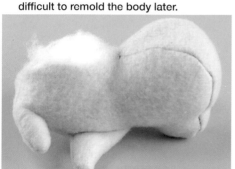

⑰ Slip-stitch the opening closed.

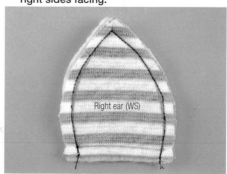

⑱ Sew the darts that you marked in step 8.

How to Stitch the Darts

1 out

3 out

2 in

⑲ Pull the thread from the dart to the bend of the legs and secure with a back-stitch to form the dog's final shape.

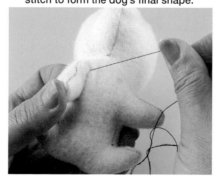

⑳ Sew the second dart and leg bend to finish the body.

3 Make the Ears

① Note: the right and left ears have different patterns.

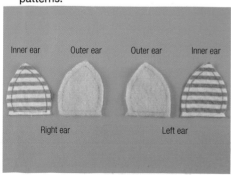

Inner ear   Outer ear   Outer ear   Inner ear

Right ear   Left ear

② Right ear: Sew Fabric A to Fabric B, with right sides facing.

Right ear (WS)

③ Turn ear right side out

④ Gather along seam allowance using a straight stitch.

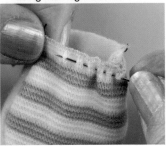

⑤ Pull the thread taut at the bottom of the ear, until the opening is ¾ inch (2 cm) at the base.

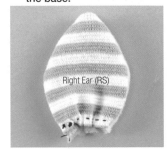

Right Ear (RS)

⑥ Fold in the seam allowance and slip-stitch the bottom.

⑦ Repeat steps 2–6 for left ear.

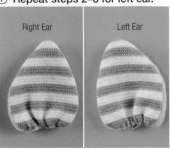

Right Ear   Left Ear

---

4 | Make the Tail

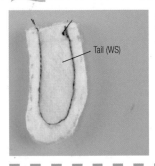

Tail (WS)

① With right sides together, back-stitch along the seam line.

② Turn right side out using a mallet or chopstick

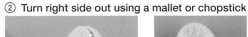

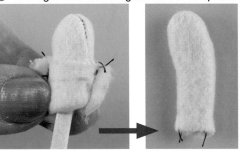

③ Fold the seam allowance and sew

Sew closed

---

5 | Attach the Ears

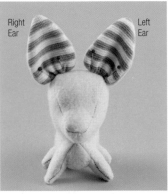

Right Ear   Left Ear

① Attach ears to body, making sure ears are symmetrical. Make sure the correct ear is on the correct side of the head.

② Sew front side of ear to the head, aligning dots.

③ Sew back of ear.

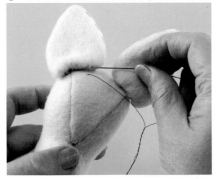

---

6 | Attach Eyes and Nose

① Mark the positions for eyes with pins.

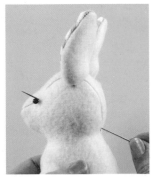

② With a double-threaded needle, make a knot. Insert needle from the back of the head to the location of the pin. The knot will be hidden in the stuffing.

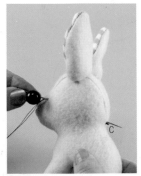

③ Attach one 11-mm button and pull the thread to the back of the head at position C. Pull the thread a bit to sink the eye into the head.

C

④ Make a French Knot (it will be on the outside of the head) and bring the needle to the location of the second pin. Attach the other eye, and pull the thread to position C.

⑤ Go back to the face, and attach an 8-mm button for nose. Pull the thread back into the head, make a knot, and hide it in the stuffing.

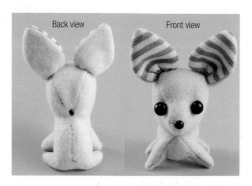

Back view   Front view

7 Attach the Tail

Sew the tail onto the back of the body at the mark on the pattern.

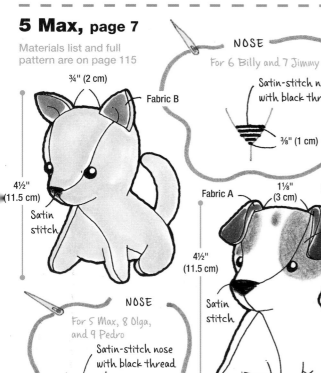

8 Finishing

Tie a ribbon around its neck

4¾ inches (12 cm) tall

Front view   Back view

---

5 Max, page 7

Materials list and full pattern are on page 115

NOSE

For 6 Billy and 7 Jimmy

Satin-stitch nose with black thread

¾" (2 cm)

Fabric B

4½" (11.5 cm)

Satin stitch

⅜" (1 cm)

NOSE

For 5 Max, 8 Olga, and 9 Pedro

Satin-stitch nose with black thread

¼" (6 mm)

⅜" (1 cm)

Fabric A   1⅛" (3 cm)   Fabric B

4½" (11.5 cm)

Satin stitch

6 Billy, page 8

Materials list and full pattern are on page 116

7 Jimmy, page 8

Materials list and full pattern are on page 117

¾" (2 cm)

Satin stitch

Add spots around eyes with black pastel

Add shading with orange pastel

All dogs are made the same way as the Chihuahua on page 45. Instructions for how to add coloring with pastels is on page 44.

Button for eye

Felt (white)

Felt and button are attached together for eye

Satin-stitch with black thread

5" (12.5 cm)

1⅛" (3 cm)

Satin stitch

Add coloring around nose with black pastel

4½" (11.5 cm)

8 Olga and 9 Pedro, page 9

Materials list and full pattern are on page 118

Add coloring with brown pastel

Pattern on page 114

MATERIALS (FOR ONE)

- 22 × 10 inches (55 × 25 cm) fleece (for Peanut) or cordlane (for Coco)
- Two ¼-inch (6 mm) buttons for eyes
- One ½-inch (13 mm) button for nose
- 12 inches (30 cm) ⅝-inch (1.5 cm) grosgrain ribbon
- Stuffing

STEP 1. SEW DARTS ON EACH OUTER BODY

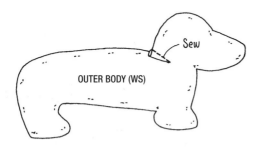

Sew

OUTER BODY (WS)

STEP 2. SEW INNER BODY

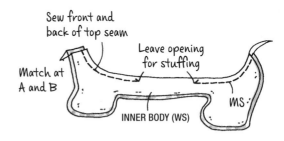

Sew front and back of top seam

Leave opening for stuffing

Match at A and B

INNER BODY (WS)

WS

STEP 3. JOIN INNER BODY AND HEAD GUSSET

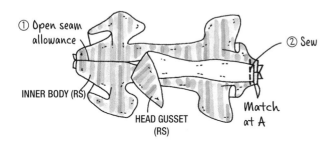

① Open seam allowance

② Sew

INNER BODY (RS)

HEAD GUSSET (RS)

Match at A

STEP 4. MAKE THE TAIL

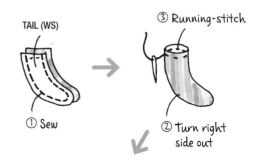

TAIL (WS)

③ Running-stitch

① Sew

② Turn right side out

④ Fold in seam allowance and pull thread to gather

STEP 5. MAKE THE EAR

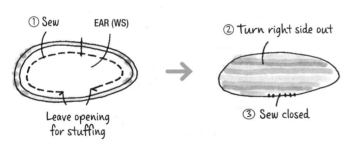

① Sew   EAR (WS)

② Turn right side out

Leave opening for stuffing

③ Sew closed

STEP 6. MAKE THE BODY

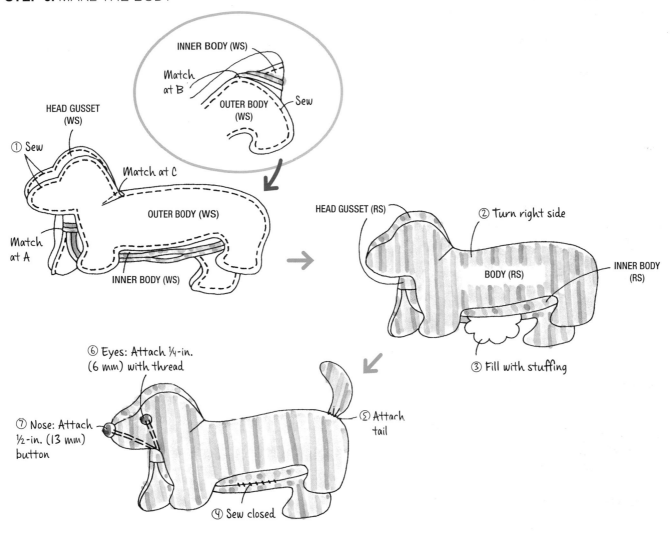

INNER BODY (WS)

Match at B

OUTER BODY (WS)

Sew

HEAD GUSSET (WS)

① Sew

Match at C

OUTER BODY (WS)

Match at A

INNER BODY (WS)

HEAD GUSSET (RS)

② Turn right side

BODY (RS)

INNER BODY (RS)

③ Fill with stuffing

⑥ Eyes: Attach ¼-in. (6 mm) with thread

⑦ Nose: Attach ½-in. (13 mm) button

④ Sew closed

⑤ Attach tail

STEP 7. FINISHING

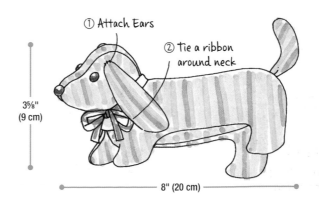

① Attach Ears

② Tie a ribbon around neck

3⅝" (9 cm)

8" (20 cm)

Pattern on page 119

Instructions for Dudley and Arthur
STEP 1. MAKE THE HEAD

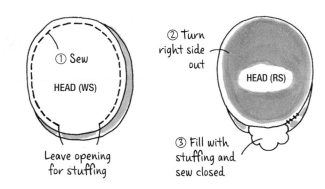

① Sew

HEAD (WS)

Leave opening for stuffing

② Turn right side out

HEAD (RS)

③ Fill with stuffing and sew closed

STEP 2. MAKE THE BODY

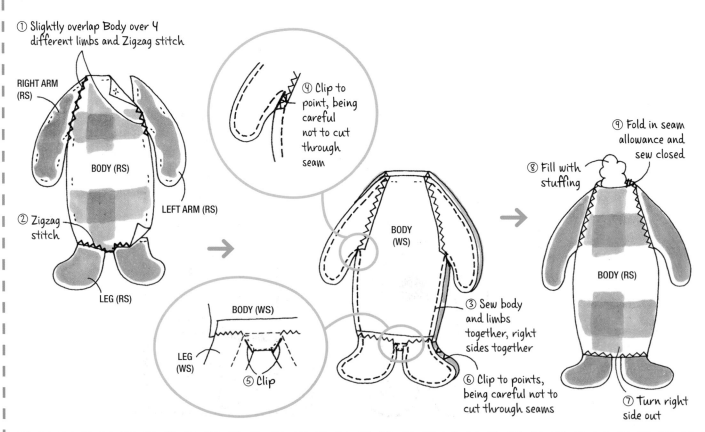

① Slightly overlap Body over 4 different limbs and Zigzag stitch

RIGHT ARM (RS)

BODY (RS)

LEFT ARM (RS)

② Zigzag stitch

LEG (RS)

④ Clip to point, being careful not to cut through seam

BODY (WS)

LEG (WS)

⑤ Clip

BODY (WS)

③ Sew body and limbs together, right sides together

⑥ Clip to points, being careful not to cut through seams

⑦ Turn right side out

⑧ Fill with stuffing

⑨ Fold in seam allowance and sew closed

BODY (RS)

STEP 3. JOIN HEAD, EARS, AND BODY

FINISHING DUDLEY

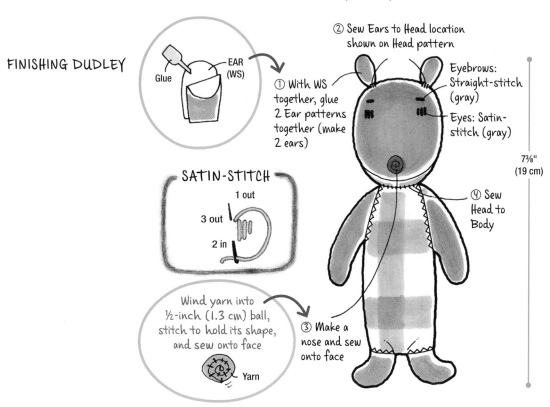

② Sew Ears to Head location shown on Head pattern

① With WS together, glue 2 Ear patterns together (make 2 ears)

Glue

EAR (WS)

Eyebrows: Straight-stitch (gray)

Eyes: Satin-stitch (gray)

7⅜" (19 cm)

SATIN-STITCH

1 out
3 out
2 in

Wind yarn into ½-inch (1.3 cm) ball, stitch to hold its shape, and sew onto face

Yarn

③ Make a nose and sew onto face

④ Sew Head to Body

FINISHING ARTHUR
• Use a single thread, any stitch

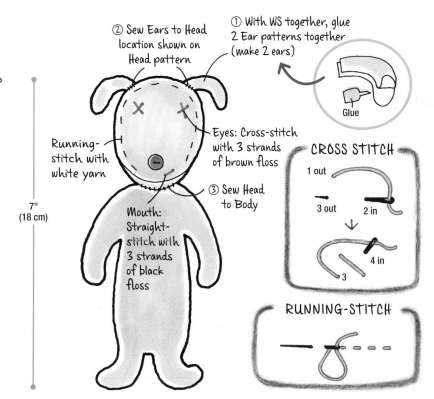

② Sew Ears to Head location shown on Head pattern

① With WS together, glue 2 Ear patterns together (make 2 ears)

Glue

Running-stitch with white yarn

Eyes: Cross-stitch with 3 strands of brown floss

③ Sew Head to Body

Mouth: Straight-stitch with 3 strands of black floss

7" (18 cm)

CROSS STITCH

1 out
3 out
2 in
4 in
3

RUNNING-STITCH

MATERIALS FOR 12 CHARLIE

- 10 × 6 inches (25 × 15 cm) brown cotton jersey, Fabric A
- 6 × 6 inches (15 × 15 cm) white cotton jersey, Fabric B
- Black yarn
- Purple yarn
- Stuffing
- Fabric marker (blue in photo)

MATERIAL FOR 13 RANDY

- 6 × 6 inches (15 × 15 cm) gray cotton jersey, Fabric A
- 10 × 6 inches (25 × 15 cm) pea-green cotton jersey, Fabric B
- Two ⅜-inch (11 mm) four-hole buttons
- Brown yarn
- Dark brown yarn
- Red thread
- Stuffing

Instructions for Charlie and Randy

STEP 1. JOIN HEAD AND BODY

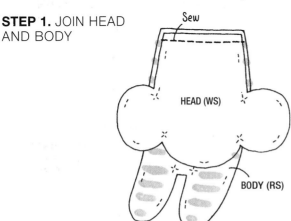

STEP 2. JOIN BODY AND ARMS

- Make Back in the same way

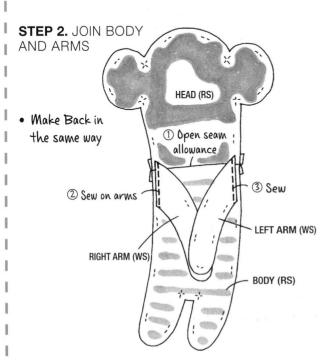

STEP 3. JOIN FRONT AND BACK

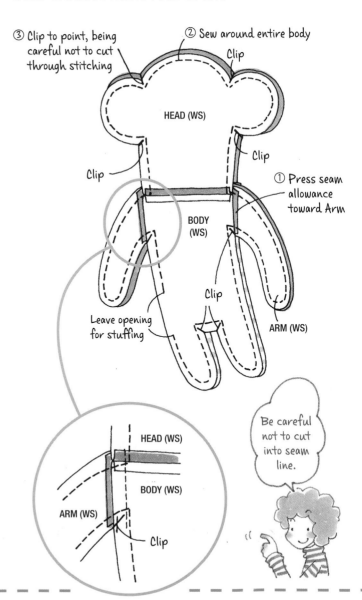

FINISHING CHARLIE

Running-stitch with purple yarn

Eyes and Nose: Satin-stitch with black yarn

6¼" (16 cm)

Mouth: Back-stitch with purple yarn

Fill with stuffing and sew closed

Draw stripes with paint marker

FINISHING RANDY

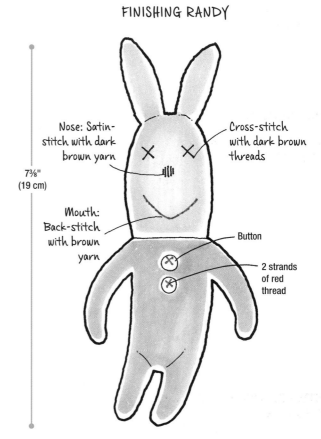

Nose: Satin-stitch with dark brown yarn

Cross-stitch with dark brown threads

Mouth: Back-stitch with brown yarn

Button

2 strands of red thread

7⅜" (19 cm)

SATIN STITCH

1 out

3 out

2 in

RUNNING-STITCH

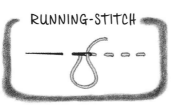

BACK STITCH

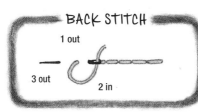

1 out

3 out

2 in

CROSS STITCH

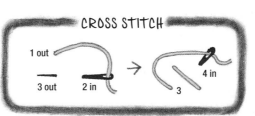

1 out

3 out

2 in

3

4 in

Note: 14 Snowy's body is one piece. 15 Cupcake's head and lower body are seamed together. Pattern on page 121

Instructions for Snowy and Cupcake

MATERIALS FOR 14 SNOWY

- 6 × 10 inches (15 × 25 cm) solid-colored terrycloth, Fabric A
- 4 × 8 inches (10 × 20 cm) striped cotton, Fabric B
- 2 × 2 inches (5 × 5 cm) pea-green felt
- Embroidery floss, brown and red
- stuffing

MATERIALS FOR 15 CUPCAKE

- 2 × 6 inches (5 × 15 cm) orange terrycloth, Fabric A
- 6 × 6 inches (15 × 15 cm) pink terrycloth, Fabric B
- Seventeen 2-inch (5 cm) white self-adhesive felt stickers
- Brown yarn
- Purple yarn
- Stuffing

STEP 1. JOIN HEAD AND BODY   **STEP 2.** MAKE ARMS

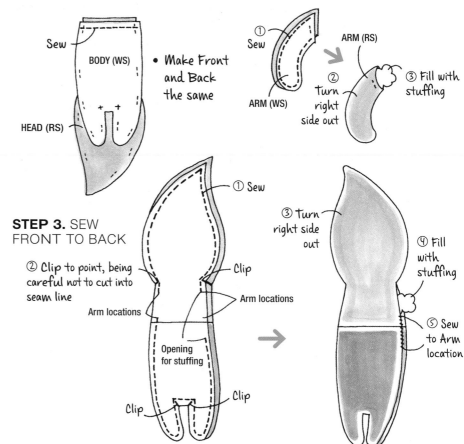

STEP 3. SEW FRONT TO BACK

② Clip to point, being careful not to cut into seam line

STEP 4. ATTACH ARMS

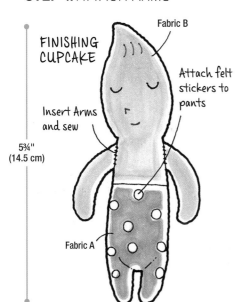

FINISHING CUPCAKE

Fabric B

Attach felt stickers to pants

Insert Arms and sew

Fabric A

5¾" (14.5 cm)

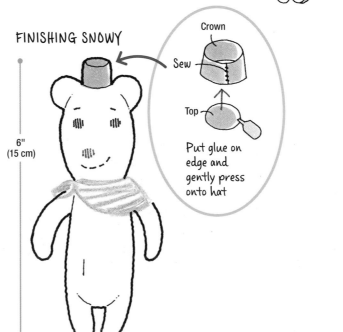

FINISHING SNOWY

6" (15 cm)

Crown

Sew

Top

Put glue on edge and gently press onto hat

Instructions for 16 Paula and 17 Howie, page 14

Pattern on page 122

MATERIALS

for Body

- 6 × 6 inches (15 × 15 cm) cotton, Fabric A (for Head)
- 8 × 6 inches (20 × 15 cm) cotton, Fabric B (for Body)
- Two 4 × 4 inches (10 × 10 cm) cotton, Fabrics C and D (for Arms)
- Two 4 × 4 inches (10 × 10 cm) cotton, Fabrics E and F (for Legs)
- Two 4 × 4 inches (10 × 10 cm) cotton, Fabrics G and H (for Socks)
- Two 4 × 2 inches (10 × 5 cm) cotton, Fabrics I and J (for Hand)
- Two 2 × 2 inches (5 × 5 cm) cotton, Fabrics K and L (for Ear)
- Two ⅜-inch (10 mm) buttons for eyes
- Dark brown yarn
- Stuffing

16 Paula's Skirt

- 4 × 8 inches (10 × 20 cm) cotton
- 4 × 8 inches (10 × 20 cm) lace

16 Paula's Apron

- 2 × 2 inch (5 × 5 cm) cotton
- 11 inches (27 cm) ⅛-inch (3 mm) satin ribbon

16 Paula's Scarf and Hat

- 6 × 1½ inches (15 × 4 cm) cotton
- 2 × ⅝-inch (5 × 1 cm) lace

16 Paula's Bag

- 2 × 2 inches (5 × 5 cm) red felt
- Scrap of cotton
- Embroidery floss, red and white

17 Howie's Pants

- 12 × 4 inches (30 × 10 cm) corduroy
- Scrap of gray felt
- Two ⅜-inch (1 cm) four-hole buttons
- Embroidery floss, pink
- 12 inches (30 cm) linen cord (for suspenders)

17 Howie's Scarf

- 6 × 1½ inches (15 × 4 cm) cotton

Instruction for Paula and Howie

STEP 1. MAKE THE HEAD

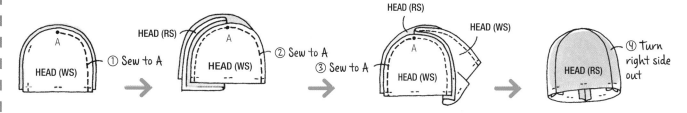

STEP 2. MAKE THE BODY AND ATTACH THE HEAD

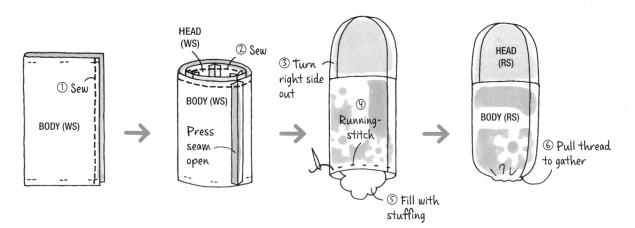

Instructions **57**

STEP 3. MAKE EARS

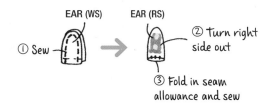

EAR (WS)   EAR (RS)

① Sew   ② Turn right side out

③ Fold in seam allowance and sew

STEP 4. MAKE THE ARMS AND LEGS   • Make Legs the same way as the Arms

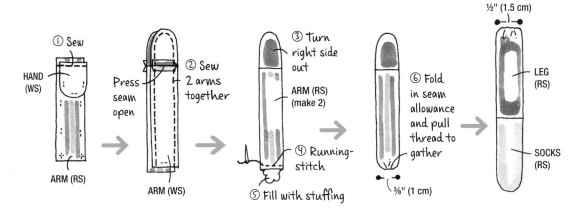

① Sew

HAND (WS)

ARM (RS)

② Sew 2 arms together

Press seam open

ARM (WS)

③ Turn right side out

ARM (RS) (make 2)

④ Running-stitch

⑤ Fill with stuffing

⑥ Fold in seam allowance and pull thread to gather

⅜" (1 cm)

½" (1.5 cm)

LEG (RS)

SOCKS (RS)

STEP 5. ATTACH THE ARMS, LEGS, AND EARS

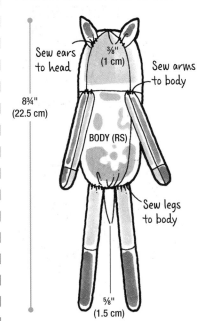

Sew ears to head

⅜" (1 cm)

Sew arms to body

8¾" (22.5 cm)

BODY (RS)

Sew legs to body

⅝" (1.5 cm)

FINISH & DRESS PAULA

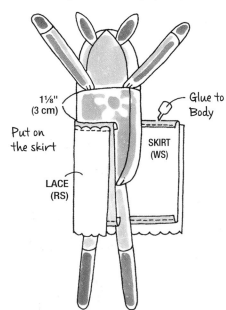

1⅛" (3 cm)

Put on the skirt

Glue to Body

SKIRT (WS)

LACE (RS)

INSTRUCTIONS FOR SKIRT

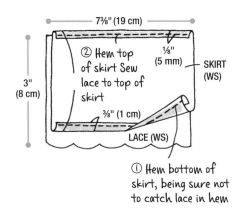

7⅜" (19 cm)

② Hem top of skirt Sew lace to top of skirt

⅛" (5 mm)

SKIRT (WS)

3" (8 cm)

⅜" (1 cm)

LACE (WS)

① Hem bottom of skirt, being sure not to catch lace in hem

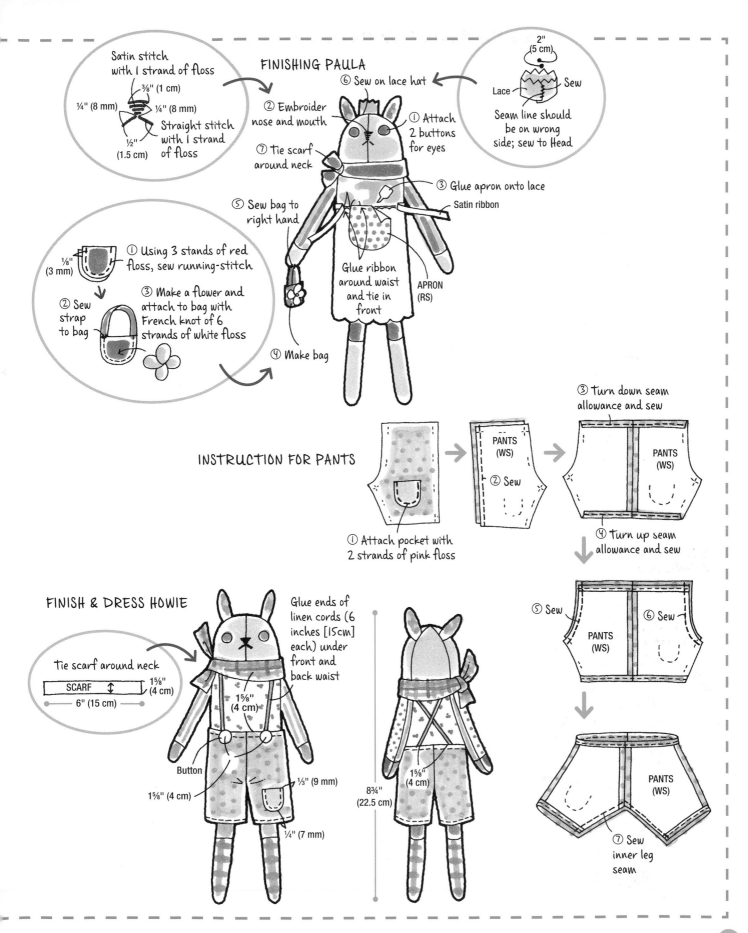

FINISHING PAULA

Satin stitch with 1 strand of floss
⅜" (1 cm)
¼" (8 mm) ¼" (8 mm)
Straight stitch with 1 strand of floss
½" (1.5 cm)

2" (5 cm)
Lace   Sew
Seam line should be on wrong side; sew to Head

⑥ Sew on lace hat
② Embroider nose and mouth
① Attach 2 buttons for eyes
⑦ Tie scarf around neck
③ Glue apron onto lace
Satin ribbon
⑤ Sew bag to right hand
Glue ribbon around waist and tie in front
APRON (RS)

⅛" (3 mm)
① Using 3 stands of red floss, sew running-stitch
② Sew strap to bag
③ Make a flower and attach to bag with French knot of 6 strands of white floss
④ Make bag

INSTRUCTION FOR PANTS

① Attach pocket with 2 strands of pink floss

PANTS (WS)
② Sew

③ Turn down seam allowance and sew
PANTS (WS)

④ Turn up seam allowance and sew

⑤ Sew   ⑥ Sew
PANTS (WS)

⑦ Sew inner leg seam
PANTS (WS)

FINISH & DRESS HOWIE

Tie scarf around neck
SCARF   1⅝" (4 cm)
6" (15 cm)

Glue ends of linen cords (6 inches [15cm] each) under front and back waist

1⅝" (4 cm)
Button
1⅝" (4 cm)   ⅓" (9 mm)
¼" (7 mm)

8¾" (22.5 cm)
1⅝" (4 cm)

MATERIALS FOR 18 HUANG HUANG

- 4 × 6 inches (10 × 15 cm) cotton print
- 8 × 4 inches (20 × 10 cm) white felt
- 4 × 4 inches (10 × 10 cm) black felt
- 2 × ¾ inches (5 × 2 cm) red felt
- Scrap of brown felt
- Scrap of white faux leather
- Two ⅛-inch (3 mm) buttons for eyes
- Two ¼-inch (6 mm) two-hole buttons to attach arms
- Embroidery floss, black
- Stuffing
- Craft glue

MATERIALS FOR 19 HONEY AND 20 MINOU (FOR ONE)

- 4 × 6 inches (10 × 15 cm) cotton print, Fabric A
- 4 × 2 inches (10 × 5 cm) cotton check, Fabric B
- 8 × 6 inches (20 × 15 cm) felt (19=gray, 20=light brown [these are for ears]
- Scrap of off-white felt
- 4 × ¾ inches (5 × 2 cm) felt (19=gray, 20=red)
- Scrap of brown felt
- Scrap of white faux leather
- Two ⅛-inch (3 mm) buttons for eyes
- Two ¼-inch (6 mm) two-hole buttons to attach arms
- Two ⅛-inch (3 mm) two-hole buttons for clothes
- Embroidery floss, black
- Stuffing
- Craft glue

STEP 1. MAKE THE ARMS AND LEGS

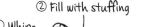
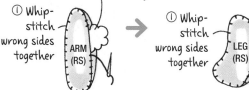

STEP 2. MAKE THE EARS

STEP 3. MAKE THE BODY

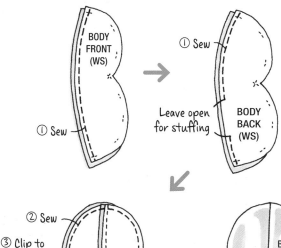

STEP 4. JOIN ARMS, LEGS, AND EARS TO BODY

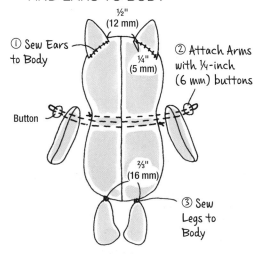

STEP 5. MAKE FACE AND PUT ON CLOTHES

FINISHING HENRY

• Use 2 strands of floss for facial features

³⁄₈" (1 cm)   ½" (12 mm)   ⅔" (15 mm)

Fly stitch

Red felt

4" (10 cm)

⅛-inch (3 mm) button

FINISHING MINOU

⅓" (7 mm)   ⅔" (15 mm)

⅛" (4 mm)   ¹⁄₁₆" (2 mm)

Irises of eyes (button)

Whites of eyes (artificial leather)

FINISHING HUANG HUANG

Whiskers: Straight stitch

½" (12 mm)

Mouth: Fly stitch

4¼" (10.5 cm)

⅛-inch (3 mm) button

Red felt

Whip stitch

³⁄₈" (1 cm)

Fly stitch

Black felt

Whip stitch

Red felt

4" (10 cm)

⅛-inch (3 mm) button

¼" (5 mm)   ⅓" (8 mm)

⅖" (7 mm)   ⅓" (8 mm)

¾" (18 mm)

19, 20 INSTRUCTIONS FOR DRESS

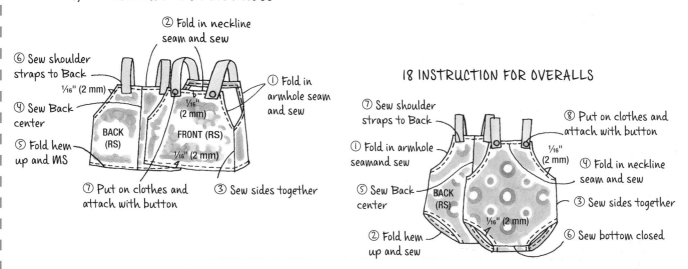

② Fold in neckline seam and sew

⑥ Sew shoulder straps to Back

¹⁄₁₆" (2 mm)

④ Sew Back center

⑤ Fold hem up and MS

① Fold in armhole seam and sew

¹⁄₁₆" (2 mm)

BACK (RS)   FRONT (RS)

¹⁄₁₆" (2 mm)

⑦ Put on clothes and attach with button

③ Sew sides together

18 INSTRUCTION FOR OVERALLS

⑦ Sew shoulder straps to Back

① Fold in armhole seam and sew

⑤ Sew Back center

② Fold hem up and sew

BACK (RS)

¹⁄₁₆" (2 mm)

⑧ Put on clothes and attach with button

¹⁄₁₆" (2 mm)

④ Fold in neckline seam and sew

③ Sew sides together

⑥ Sew bottom closed

MATERIALS FOR 21 TOBY

- 8 × 6 inches (20 × 15 cm) moss green felt (for Head, Feet, Arms)
- 4 × 2 inches (10 × 5 cm) brown felt (for Nose and Ears)
- 4 × 2 inches (10 × 5 cm) black felt (for Hat)
- 6 × 2 inches (15 × 5 cm) cotton print (for Body)
- 6 × 2 inches (15 × 5 cm) cotton solid (for Pants)
- Two ¼-inch (6 mm) black felt stickers for irises
- Two ⅜-inch (9 mm) white circles of fabric adhesive for eyes
- 7 inches (18 cm) ⅝-inch (1 cm) velvet ribbon for necktie
- 2 inches (5 cm) ¼-inch (6 mm) grosgrain ribbon for hat
- Embroidery floss, red
- Stuffing
- Craft glue

MATERIALS FOR 22 GIGI

- 8 × 6 inches (20 × 15 cm) bright yellow felt (for Head, Feet, Arms, Ears)
- 2 × 2 inches (5 × 5 cm) light blue felt (for Hat)
- 2 × 2 inches (5 × 5 cm) orange felt (for Nose)
- 6 × 2 inches (15 × 5 cm) cotton print (for Body)
- 6 × 2 inches (15 × 5 cm) cotton solid (for Pants)
- Two ¼-inch (6 mm) black felt stickers for eyes
- Two ⅝-inch (9 mm) white fabric adhesive circles for eyes
- 3 inches (7 cm) ⅝-inch (1 cm) wide satin ribbon
- One ⅓-inch (8 mm) white pom-pom for hat
- Embroidery floss, red
- Stuffing
- Craft glue

MATERIALS FOR 23 KATE

- 10 × 6 inches (25 × 15 cm) dark pink felt (for Head, Feet, Arms, Ears)
- 2 × 2 inches (5 × 5 cm) cream felt (for Nose)
- Scrap of purple felt (for Flower)
- 6 × 2 inches (15 × 5 cm) cotton print (for Body)
- 6 × 2 inches (15 × 5 cm) cotton solid (for Pants)
- Two ¼-inch (6 mm) dark blue felt stickers for the eyes
- One ¼-inch (6 mm) black felt sticker for the nose
- One ⅜-inch (9 mm) orange felt sticker for flower
- Two ¼-inch (6 mm) white fabric adhesive circles
- 8½ inches (22 cm) ¼-inch (6 mm) velvet ribbon
- Embroidery floss, red
- Stuffing
- Craft glue

STEP 1. MAKE THE HEAD

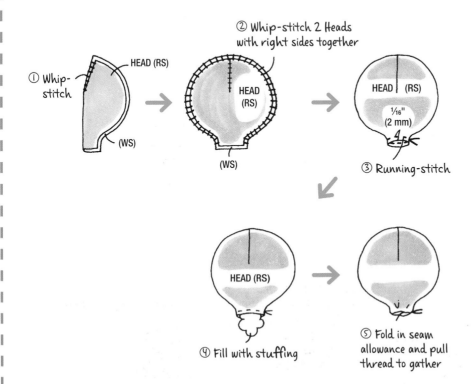

① Whip-stitch

HEAD (RS)

(WS)

② Whip-stitch 2 Heads with right sides together

HEAD (RS)

(WS)

HEAD (RS)

1/16" (2 mm)

③ Running-stitch

④ Fill with stuffing

HEAD (RS)

⑤ Fold in seam allowance and pull thread to gather

WHIP STITCH

STEP 2. MAKE THE BODY

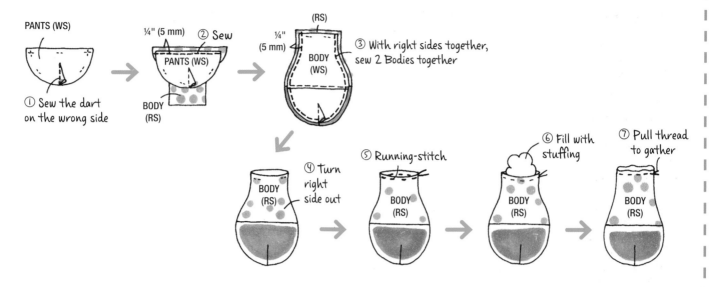

PANTS (WS)

① Sew the dart on the wrong side

¼" (5 mm) ② Sew

PANTS (WS)

BODY (RS)

(RS)

¼" (5 mm)

BODY (WS)

③ With right sides together, sew 2 Bodies together

④ Turn right side out

BODY (RS)

⑤ Running-stitch

BODY (RS)

⑥ Fill with stuffing

BODY (RS)

⑦ Pull thread to gather

BODY (RS)

STEP 3. MAKE THE ARMS

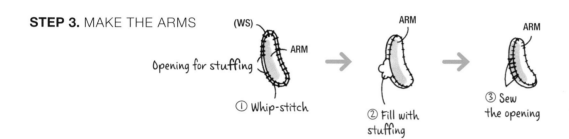

(WS)

ARM

Opening for stuffing

① Whip-stitch

ARM

② Fill with stuffing

ARM

③ Sew the opening

STEP 4. MAKE THE FEET

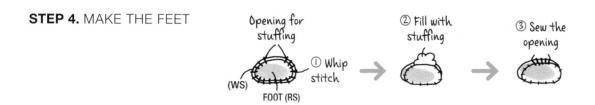

Opening for stuffing

① Whip stitch

(WS)

FOOT (RS)

② Fill with stuffing

③ Sew the opening

STEP 5. MAKE THE HAT

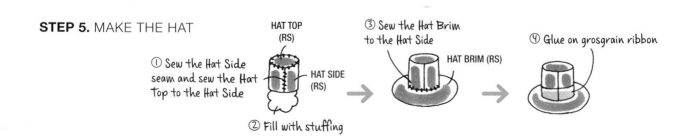

① Sew the Hat Side seam and sew the Hat Top to the Hat Side

HAT TOP (RS)

HAT SIDE (RS)

② Fill with stuffing

③ Sew the Hat Brim to the Hat Side

HAT BRIM (RS)

④ Glue on grosgrain ribbon

STEP 6. MAKE THE FACE

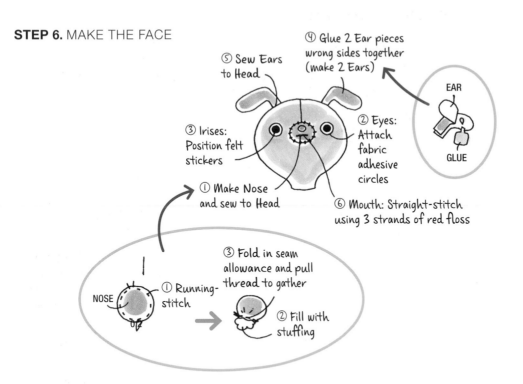

⑤ Sew Ears to Head

④ Glue 2 Ear pieces wrong sides together (make 2 Ears)

EAR

GLUE

③ Irises: Position felt stickers

② Eyes: Attach fabric adhesive circles

① Make Nose and sew to Head

⑥ Mouth: Straight-stitch using 3 strands of red floss

NOSE

① Running-stitch

③ Fold in seam allowance and pull thread to gather

② Fill with stuffing

STEP 7. ATTACH ARMS, FEET, FACE, AND HAT

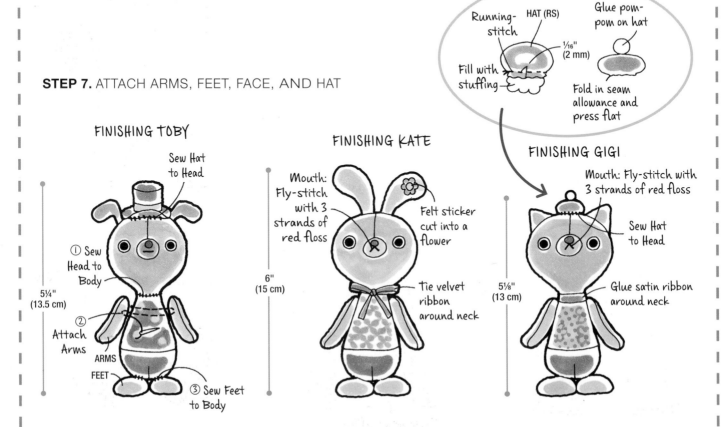

Running-stitch

HAT (RS)

Glue pom-pom on hat

1/16" (2 mm)

Fill with stuffing

Fold in seam allowance and press flat

FINISHING TOBY

Sew Hat to Head

① Sew Head to Body

② Attach Arms

ARMS

FEET

③ Sew Feet to Body

5¼" (13.5 cm)

FINISHING KATE

Mouth: Fly-stitch with 3 strands of red floss

Felt sticker cut into a flower

Tie velvet ribbon around neck

6" (15 cm)

FINISHING GIGI

Mouth: Fly-stitch with 3 strands of red floss

Sew Hat to Head

Glue satin ribbon around neck

5⅛" (13 cm)

Pattern on page 125

STEP 1. MAKE THE HEAD

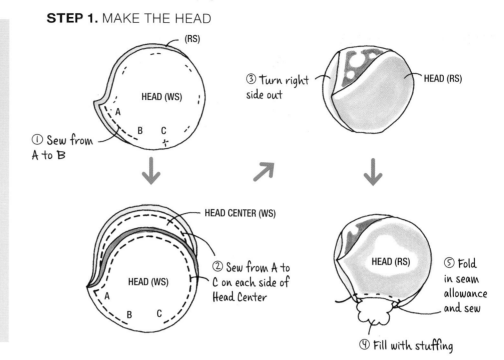

MATERIALS (FOR ONE)

- 10 × 8 inches (20 × 25 cm) solid-colored faux leather, Fabric A
- 8 × 8 inches (20 × 20 cm) polka-dotted cotton, Fabric B
- 4 inches (10 cm) feather boa (for 24 Fawn)
- ¾ × 8 inches (2 × 20 cm) white faux rabbit fur (for 25 Pony)
- 2 × 1 inches (5 × 3 cm) emerald green felt
- 2 × ⅝ inches (6 × 1 cm) black faux leather
- One ⅓ inch (8 mm) pom-pom
- 16 inches (40 cm) 19-gauge wire
- Stuffing

(RS)

HEAD (WS)

A
B C

① Sew from A to B

HEAD CENTER (WS)

HEAD (WS)

A
B C

② Sew from A to C on each side of Head Center

③ Turn right side out

HEAD (RS)

HEAD (RS)

⑤ Fold in seam allowance and sew

④ Fill with stuffing

STEP 2. MAKE THE BODY

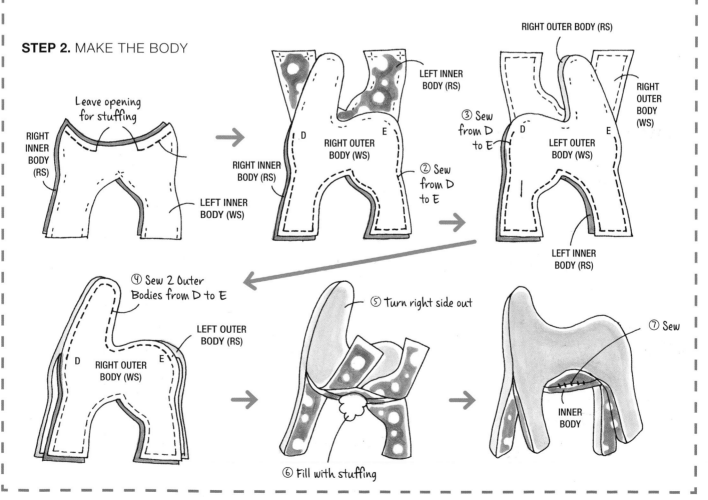

Leave opening for stuffing

RIGHT INNER BODY (RS)

LEFT INNER BODY (WS)

LEFT INNER BODY (RS)

RIGHT INNER BODY (RS)

RIGHT OUTER BODY (WS)

D E

② Sew from D to E

RIGHT OUTER BODY (RS)

③ Sew from D to E

LEFT OUTER BODY (WS)

D E

RIGHT OUTER BODY (WS)

LEFT INNER BODY (RS)

④ Sew 2 Outer Bodies from D to E

LEFT OUTER BODY (RS)

RIGHT OUTER BODY (WS)

D E

⑤ Turn right side out

⑥ Fill with stuffing

⑦ Sew

INNER BODY

STEP 3. ATTACH BODY TO THE HEAD

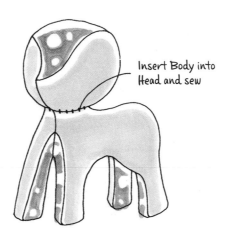

Insert Body into Head and sew

STEP 4. MAKE EARS AND ATTACH

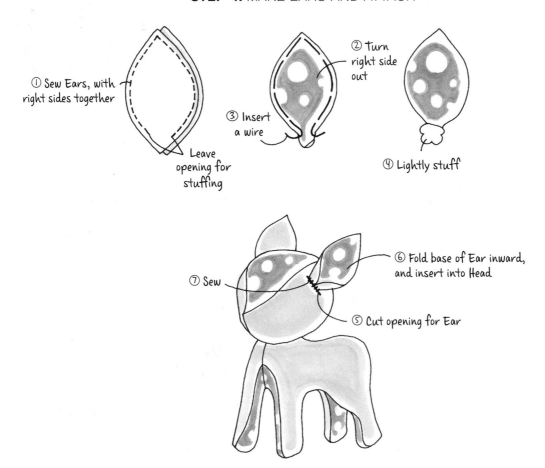

① Sew Ears, with right sides together

Leave opening for stuffing

③ Insert a wire

② turn right side out

④ Lightly stuff

⑥ Fold base of Ear inward, and insert into Head

⑦ Sew

⑤ Cut opening for Ear

FINISHING FAWN

Glue Eyes and Eyelashes to Head

Glue pom-pom for nose

6⅛" (15.5 cm)

Wrap boa around neck and glue

4" (10 cm)

TAIL

Attach tail the same way as the ears

Cut opening for Tail

⅜" (1 cm)

⅛" (4 mm)

FINISHING PONY

Cut 3½ × ¾ inches (9 × 2 cm) fur for Head

Glue fur on Body Center

Glue pom-pom for nose

Fold remaining fur in half and attach same as Fawn's Tail

6⅛" (15.5 cm)

Glue Eyes and Eyelashes to Head

Tail is 2¼ × ¾ inches (5 × 2 cm)

5¼" (13.5 cm)

INSTRUCTIONS FOR TAG

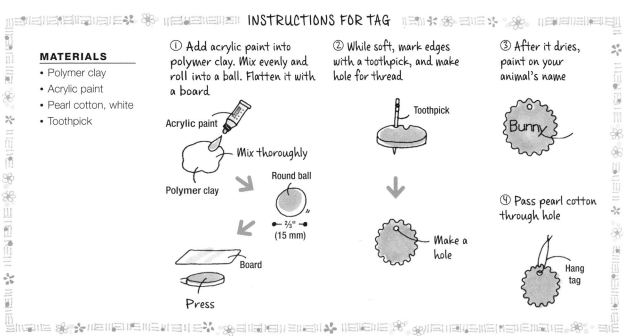

MATERIALS
- Polymer clay
- Acrylic paint
- Pearl cotton, white
- Toothpick

① Add acrylic paint into polymer clay. Mix evenly and roll into a ball. Flatten it with a board

Acrylic paint

Mix thoroughly

Polymer clay

Round ball

⅔" (15 mm)

Board

Press

② While soft, mark edges with a toothpick, and make hole for thread

Toothpick

Make a hole

③ After it dries, paint on your animal's name

Bunny

④ Pass pearl cotton through hole

Hang tag

MATERIALS FOR 26 BUNNY

- 12 × 6 inches (30 × 15 cm) light blue faux fur
- 10 × 2 inches (25 × 5 cm) polka-dotted cotton, Fabric A
- 4 × 2 inches (10 × 5 cm) white boa, Fabric B
- 2 × 2 inches (5 × 5 cm) white faux fur, Fabric C
- 2 × 2 inches (5 × 5 cm) emerald green felt
- 2 × ⅜ inches (6 × 1 cm) black faux leather
- One ¼-inch (6 mm) pink pom-pom
- Two ⅜-inch (11 mm) white pom-poms
- 18 inches (45 cm) 19-gauge wire
- Stuffing
- Craft glue

Instruction for Bunny

STEP 1. MAKE THE HEAD

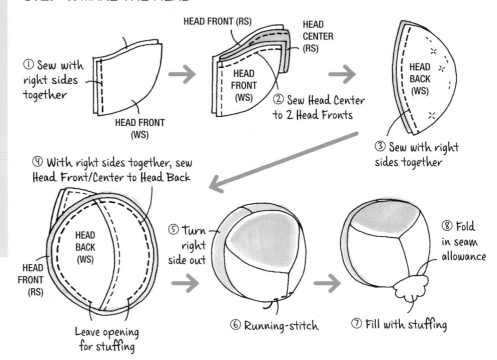

STEP 2. MAKE THE BODY

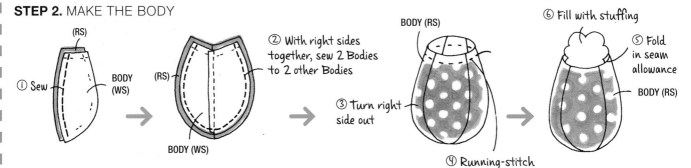

STEP 3. MAKE THE LEGS

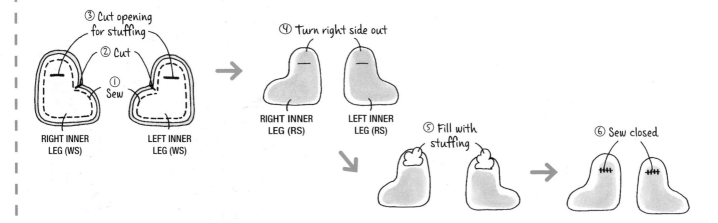

STEP 4. MAKE THE ARMS

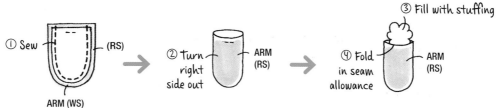

① Sew (RS) ARM (WS)

② turn right side out ARM (RS)

③ Fill with stuffing

④ Fold in seam allowance ARM (RS)

STEP 5. MAKE THE EARS

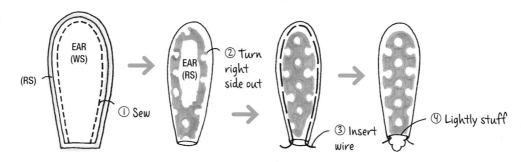

EAR (WS) (RS) ① Sew

EAR (RS) ② turn right side out

③ Insert wire

④ Lightly stuff

STEP 6. MAKE THE TAIL

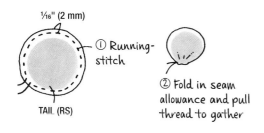

¹⁄₁₆" (2 mm)

① Running-stitch

TAIL (RS)

② Fold in seam allowance and pull thread to gather

STEP 7. JOIN ARMS, LEGS, AND HEAD TO BODY

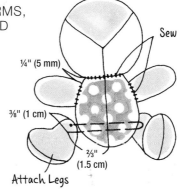

Sew

¼" (5 mm)

⅜" (1 cm)

⅔" (1.5 cm)

Attach Legs

STEP 8. ATTACH EARS AND TAIL

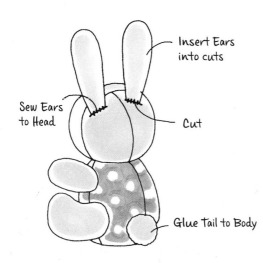

Insert Ears into cuts

Sew Ears to Head

Cut

Glue Tail to Body

FINISHING BUNNY

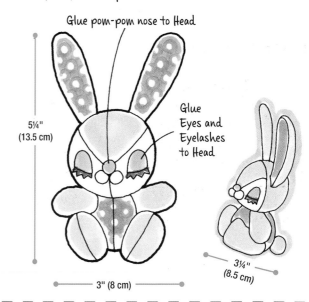

Glue pom-pom nose to Head

5¼" (13.5 cm)

Glue Eyes and Eyelashes to Head

3" (8 cm)

3¼" (8.5 cm)

MATERIALS FOR 27 SQUIRREL

- 12 × 6 inches (30 × 15 cm) orange felt
- 4 × 8 inches (10 × 20 cm) faux fur, Fabric A
- 4 × 4 inches (10 × 10 cm) brown faux leather, Fabric B
- 4 × 2 inches (10 × 5 cm) cotton flowered print, Fabric C
- 2 × 1 inches (5 × 3 cm) white felt
- 2 × 2 inches (5 × 5 cm) emerald green felt
- 2 × 1 inches (5 × 2 cm) black felt
- One ⅓-inch (8 mm) orange pom-pom
- Two ⅜-inch (11 mm) white pom-poms
- 22 inches (55 cm) 19-gauge wire
- Pearl cotton, black
- Stuffing
- Craft glue

STEP 5. MAKE THE TAIL

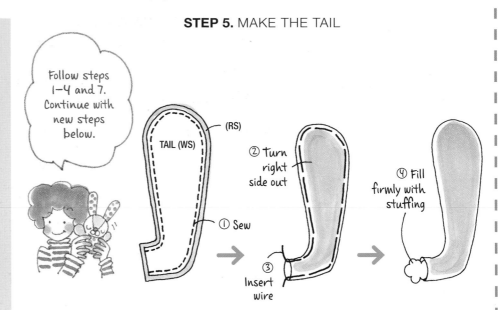

Follow steps 1–4 and 7. Continue with new steps below.

TAIL (WS)

(RS)

① Sew

③ Insert wire

② turn right side out

④ Fill firmly with stuffing

STEP 6. MAKE THE EARS

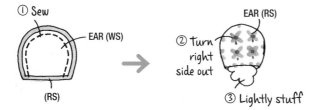

① Sew

EAR (WS)

(RS)

EAR (RS)

② turn right side out

③ Lightly stuff

STEP 8. ATTACH EARS AND TAIL TO BODY

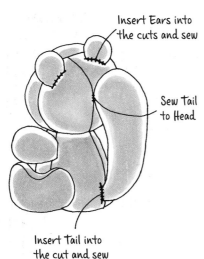

Insert Ears into the cuts and sew

Sew Tail to Head

Insert Tail into the cut and sew

FINISHING SQUIRREL

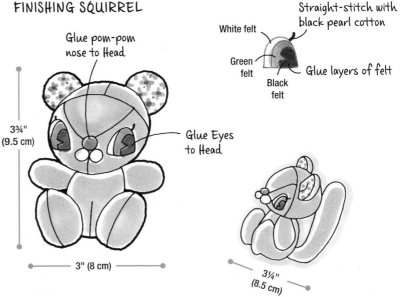

Glue pom-pom nose to Head

Glue Eyes to Head

3¾" (9.5 cm)

3" (8 cm)

3¼" (8.5 cm)

White felt

Green felt

Black felt

Straight-stitch with black pearl cotton

Glue layers of felt

MATERIALS FOR 28 ANDERS

- 8 × 6 inches (20 × 15 cm) dark blue flannel
- 2 × 2 inches (5 × 5 cm) cream flannel
- 4 × 2 inches (10 × 5 cm) pea green felt
- 4 × 4 inches (10 × 10 cm) purple felt
- 2 × 2 inches (5 × 5 cm) orange felt
- 4 × 6 inches (10 × 15 cm) dark brown felt
- 5 × ¼ inches (13 cm × 6 mm) bright yellow felt
- Scraps of brown, cream, red, light blue, and white felt
- Four ⅜-inch (11 mm) joint sets
- 6 × 2 inches (15 × 6 cm) cardboard
- Embroidery floss, yellow
- Stuffing
- Awl
- Craft glue

MATERIALS FOR 29 ZOE

- 8 × 6 inches (20 × 15 cm) off-white felt
- 4 × 4 inches (10 × 10 cm) blue felt
- 2 × 2 inches (5 × 5 cm) bright yellow felt
- 4 × 6 inches (10 × 15 cm) dark brown felt
- 8 × 6 inches (20 × 15 cm) orange felt
- 4 × 2 inches (11 × 5 cm) pink felt
- Scraps of brown, cream, and red felt
- Two ¼-inch (6 mm) white felt stickers
- Two ⅛-inch (5 mm) black felt stickers
- Four ⅜-inch (11 mm) joint sets
- 6 × 2 inches (15 × 6 cm) thick paper
- Embroidery floss, blue, black, dark brown, pea green
- Stuffing
- Awl
- Craft glue

Instruction for 28 Anders

STEP 1. MAKE THE HEAD

• Blanket-stitch with 2 strands of floss

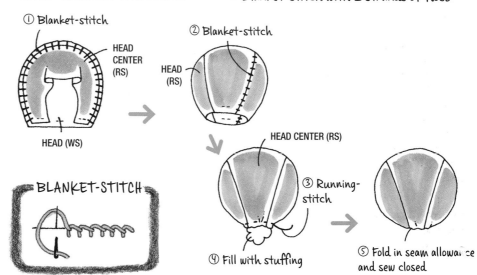

STEP 2. MAKE THE BODY

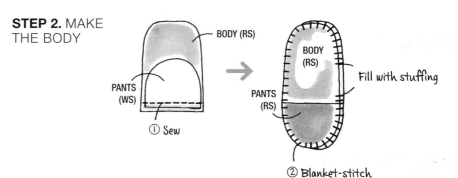

STEP 3. MAKE THE ARMS

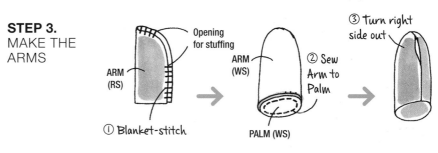

STEP 4. MAKE THE LEGS

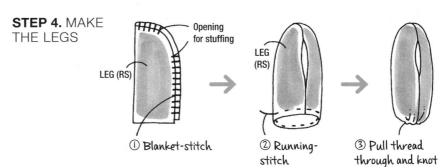

STEP 5. MAKE THE MUZZLE AND NOSE

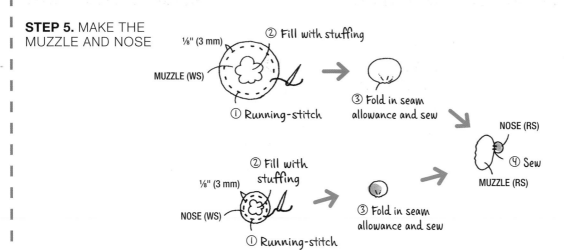

⅛" (3 mm)

② Fill with stuffing

MUZZLE (WS)

① Running-stitch

③ Fold in seam allowance and sew

NOSE (RS)

④ Sew

MUZZLE (RS)

⅛" (3 mm)

② Fill with stuffing

NOSE (WS)

① Running-stitch

③ Fold in seam allowance and sew

STEP 6. MAKE THE EARS

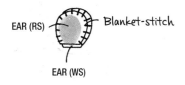

EAR (RS)

Blanket-stitch

EAR (WS)

STEP 7. ATTACH EARS, EYES, AND NOSE TO HEAD

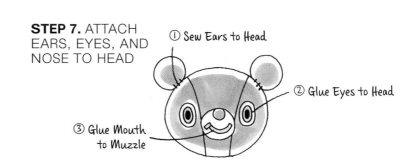

① Sew Ears to Head

② Glue Eyes to Head

③ Glue Mouth to Muzzle

STEP 8. MAKE HOLES FOR JOINTS

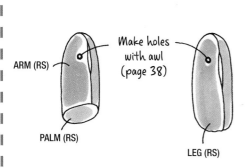

ARM (RS)

Make holes with awl (page 38)

PALM (RS)

LEG (RS)

BODY (RS)

Make holes with awl (page 38)

STEP 9. PUT JOINT IN ARMS AND LEGS

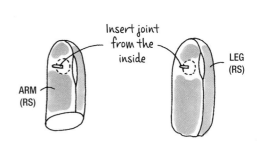

Insert joint from the inside

ARM (RS)

LEG (RS)

STEP 10. ATTACH ARMS AND LEGS TO BODY WITH JOINT

• Make sure joint is correctly placed

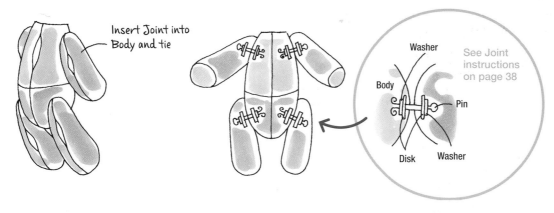

Insert Joint into Body and tie

Washer

Body

See Joint instructions on page 38

Pin

Disk   Washer

STEP 11. FILL WITH STUFFING AND SEW CLOSED

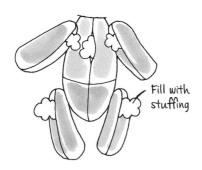

Fill with stuffing

STEP 12. JOIN BODY AND HEAD

Sew

STEP 13. MAKE SHOES

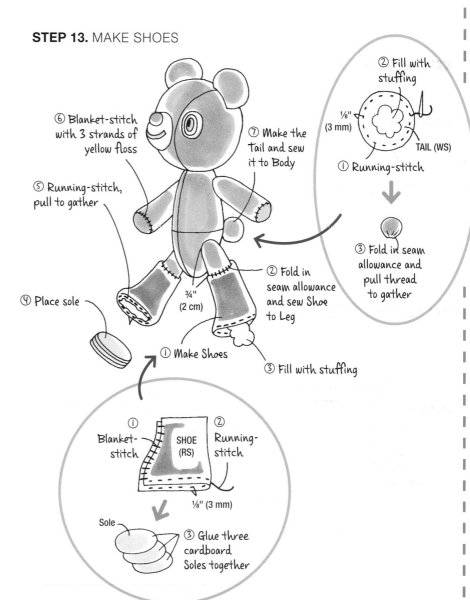

⑥ Blanket-stitch with 3 strands of yellow floss

⑦ Make the Tail and sew it to Body

⑤ Running-stitch, pull to gather

② Fill with stuffing

① Running-stitch

TAIL (WS)

⅛" (3 mm)

③ Fold in seam allowance and pull thread to gather

④ Place sole

② Fold in seam allowance and sew Shoe to Leg

¾" (2 cm)

① Make Shoes

③ Fill with stuffing

①
Blanket-stitch

SHOE (RS)

②
Running-stitch

⅛" (3 mm)

Sole

③ Glue three cardboard Soles together

FINISHING ZOE

4"
(10 cm)

¼" (5 mm)

Sew

Blanket-stitch with 6 strands of dark brown floss

(pink)

Make the bag

FINISHING ANDERS

⑨ Wrap a bright yellow scarf (5 × ¼ inch [13 cm × 6 mm]) around neck

5¾" (14.5 cm)

6¼" (16 cm)

Eyebrows: Back-stitch with 3 strands of black floss

Hang Bag on shoulder and sew to Body

1⅛" (3 cm)

Make skirt and attach

⑧ Glue Sole to Shoe

① Glue three cardboard Soles together

Sole

② Running-stitch

1/16" (3 mm)

③ Insert cardboard and pull thread to gather

Blanket-stitch with 3 strands of blue floss

FRENCH KNOT

Use 6 strands of dark brown floss

6¾" (17 cm)

1⅛" (3 cm)

Orange felt

SKIRT (RS)

× × × × × × × × ×

① Make 6 cross-stitches with pea green floss

② Sew

SKIRT (WS)

1/16" (3 mm)

③ Running-stitch

1/16" (3 mm)

× × × × ×

MATERIALS FOR 30 KENKEN

- 6 × 4 inches (15 × 10 cm) brown felt
- 2 × 2 inches (5 × 5 cm) beige felt
- Scrap of red felt
- Two ¼-inch (6 mm) white felt stickers for eyes
- Two ⅛-inch (3 mm) black felt stickers for eyes
- One ¼-inch (6 mm) button for nose
- 4 inches (10 cm) ⅛-inch (3 mm) satin ribbon
- Embroidery floss, brown
- One star-shaped bead
- Stuffing
- Craft glue

MATERIALS FOR 31 MIMI

- 6 × 4 inches (15 × 10 cm) pea green felt
- 2 × 2 inches (5 × 5 cm) beige felt
- 4 × ¾ inches (11 × 2 cm) pink felt
- Scrap of orange felt
- Two ¼-inch (6 mm) white felt stickers for eyes
- Two ⅛-inch (3 mm) black felt stickers for eyes
- One ⅓-inch (3 mm) button for nose
- Embroidery floss, pea green
- Black nylon string
- Stuffing
- Craft glue

STEP 1. MAKE THE BODY

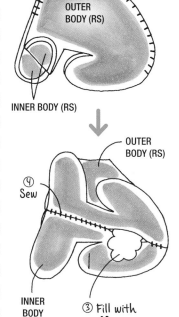

① Blanket-stitch

OUTER BODY (WS)

INNER BODY (RS)

② Blanket-stitch between marks on pattern

OUTER BODY (RS)

INNER BODY (RS)

④ Sew

OUTER BODY (RS)

INNER BODY (RS)

③ Fill with stuffing

STEP 2. MAKE THE HEAD

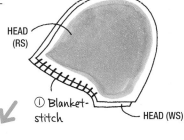

① Blanket-stitch

HEAD (RS)

HEAD (WS)

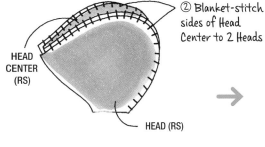

② Blanket-stitch sides of Head Center to 2 Heads

HEAD CENTER (RS)

HEAD (RS)

HEAD (RS)

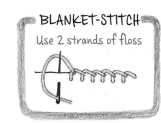

HEAD CENTER (RS)

HEAD (RS)

③ Running-stitch

④ Fill with stuffing

BLANKET-STITCH

Use 2 strands of floss

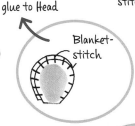

⑦ Glue Eyes to Head

⑧ Glue Nose to Head

White

Black

¼" (7 mm)

⑥ Make Ears and glue to Head

1⅛" (3 cm)

Blanket-stitch

⑤ Fold in seam allowance and sew

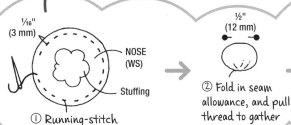

1/16" (3 mm)

NOSE (WS)

Stuffing

① Running-stitch

½" (12 mm)

② Fold in seam allowance, and pull thread to gather

③ Sew on button for Nose

④ Glue on Mouth

STEP 3. JOIN HEAD AND BODY

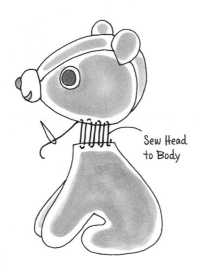

Sew Head to Body

STEP 4. ATTACH TAIL AND FINISH

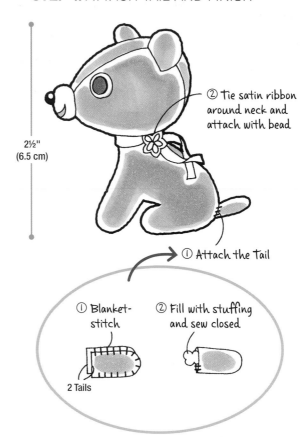

2½" (6.5 cm)

② Tie satin ribbon around neck and attach with bead

① Attach the Tail

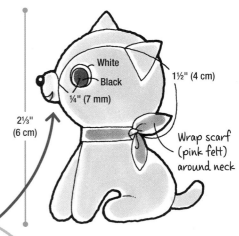

① Blanket-stitch

② Fill with stuffing and sew closed

2 Tails

MAKE THE HEAD (MIMI)

Follow steps 1, 3, and 4 for Kenken and use instructions here to make the Head.

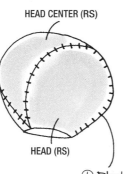

HEAD CENTER (RS)

HEAD (RS)

① Blanket-stitch

② Running-stitch

③ Fill with stuffing

FINISHING MIMI

White

Black

¼" (7 mm)

1½" (4 cm)

2⅓" (6 cm)

Wrap scarf (pink felt) around neck

INSTRUCTIONS FOR ATTACHING NOSE

Nose (WS)

1/16" (3 mm)

Running-stitch

Stuffing

Fold in seam allowance, and pull thread to gather

½" (12 mm)

Sew on button for Nose

Glue on Mouth

¼" (5 mm)

Thread nylon string for whiskers

Pattern on page 129

MATERIALS FOR 32 VIOLET

- 4 × 4 inches (10 × 10 cm) purple felt
- 2 × 2 inches (5 × 5 cm) off-white felt
- 4 × 2 inches (10 × 5 cm) green felt
- 2 × 2 inches (5 × 5 cm) cream felt
- Scrap of red felt
- Two ¼-inch (6 mm) white felt stickers
- Two ⅛-inch (3 mm) black felt stickers
- 4 × 1 inches (11 × 3 cm) striped cotton
- One ⅛-inch (3 mm) button for nose
- Embroidery floss, purple and green
- Stuffing
- Pin
- Craft glue

MATERIALS FOR 33 PALMER

- 4 × 4 inches (10 × 10 cm) pink felt
- 4 × 2 inches (10 × 5 cm) white felt
- 1 × 1 inches (3 × 3 cm) yellow felt
- Scrap of black felt
- 8 × 2 inches (20 × 5 cm) cotton print
- One ⅝-inch (1 cm) pom-pom
- 8 inches (20 cm) 19-gauge wire
- Embroidery floss, pink, yellow, blue, black, and green
- Stuffing
- Craft glue

STEP 1. FOR 32 VIOLET MAKE THE BODY

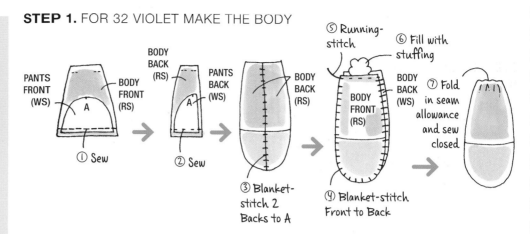

STEP 1. FOR 33 PALMER MAKE THE BODY

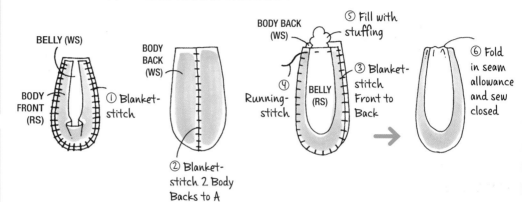

STEP 2. MAKE THE ARMS • Blanket-stitch with 2 strands of floss

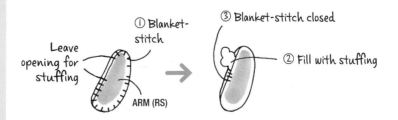

STEP 3. MAKE THE LEGS

STEP 4. MAKE THE HEAD

- The pictures show Violet's face (scallop-shaped at top) and head. The steps are the same for making Palmer's face and head.

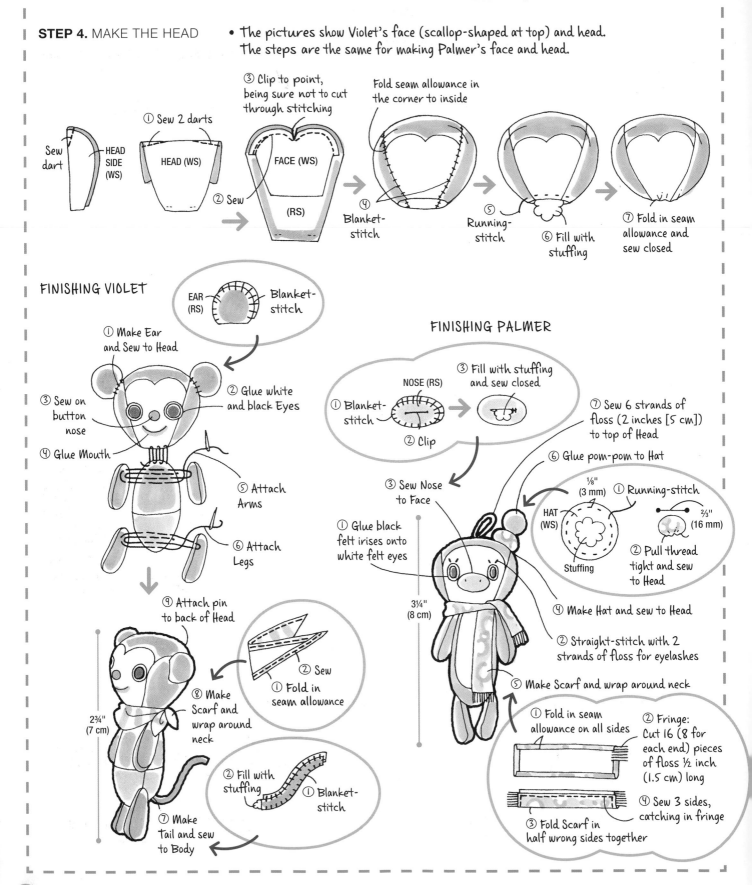

Sew dart

HEAD SIDE (WS)

① Sew 2 darts

HEAD (WS)

② Sew

③ Clip to point, being sure not to cut through stitching

FACE (WS)

(RS)

④ Blanket-stitch

Fold seam allowance in the corner to inside

⑤ Running-stitch

⑥ Fill with stuffing

⑦ Fold in seam allowance and sew closed

FINISHING VIOLET

EAR (RS) — Blanket-stitch

① Make Ear and Sew to Head

② Glue white and black Eyes

③ Sew on button nose

④ Glue Mouth

⑤ Attach Arms

⑥ Attach Legs

⑨ Attach pin to back of Head

② Sew

① Fold in seam allowance

⑧ Make Scarf and wrap around neck

2¾" (7 cm)

② Fill with stuffing

① Blanket-stitch

⑦ Make Tail and sew to Body

FINISHING PALMER

NOSE (RS)

① Blanket-stitch

② Clip

③ Fill with stuffing and sew closed

③ Sew Nose to Face

① Glue black felt irises onto white felt eyes

3¼" (8 cm)

⑦ Sew 6 strands of floss (2 inches [5 cm]) to top of Head

⑥ Glue pom-pom to Hat

⅛" (3 mm)

① Running-stitch

HAT (WS)

Stuffing

⅔" (16 mm)

② Pull thread tight and sew to Head

④ Make Hat and sew to Head

② Straight-stitch with 2 strands of floss for eyelashes

⑤ Make Scarf and wrap around neck

① Fold in seam allowance on all sides

② Fringe: Cut 16 (8 for each end) pieces of floss ½ inch (1.5 cm) long

③ Fold Scarf in half wrong sides together

④ Sew 3 sides, catching in fringe

Pattern on page 130

MATERIALS

- 4 × 6 inches (10 × 15 cm) pink felt
- 4 × ⅝ inches (10 × 1 cm) pea green felt
- 4 × 4 inches (10 × 10 cm) blue felt
- 2 × 2 inches (5 × 5 cm) white felt
- 8 × 4 inches (20 × 10 cm) light blue felt
- 4 × 2 inches (10 × 5 cm) yellow felt
- Scrap of red felt
- Two ¼-inch (6 mm) white felt stickers
- Two ⅛-inch (3 mm) black felt stickers
- Seven ¼-inch (6 mm) green felt stickers
- Embroidery floss, pink, yellow, blue, and black
- 4 inches (10 cm) pipe cleaner
- Stuffing
- Craft glue

STEP 1. MAKE THE BODY

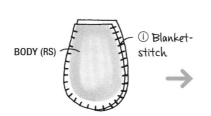

① Blanket-stitch

BODY (RS)

③ Fill with stuffing

② Running-stitch

④ Fold in seam allowance and sew closed

BLANKET-STITCH
Use 2 strands of floss

STEP 2. MAKE THE HEAD

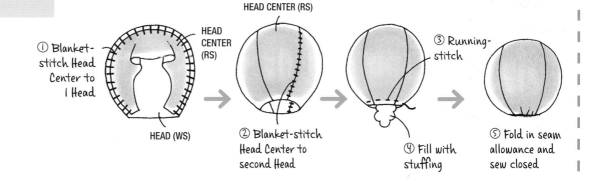

① Blanket-stitch Head Center to 1 Head

HEAD CENTER (RS)

HEAD (WS)

HEAD CENTER (RS)

② Blanket-stitch Head Center to second Head

③ Running-stitch

④ Fill with stuffing

⑤ Fold in seam allowance and sew closed

STEP 3. MAKE THE LEGS

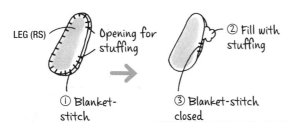

LEG (RS)

Opening for stuffing

① Blanket-stitch

② Fill with stuffing

③ Blanket-stitch closed

STEP 4. MAKE THE ARMS

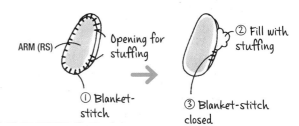

ARM (RS)

Opening for stuffing

① Blanket-stitch

② Fill with stuffing

③ Blanket-stitch closed

STEP 5. MAKE THE NOSE

NOSE (RS)
② Clip
① Blanket-stitch
④ Sew closed
③ Fill with stuffing

STEP 6. MAKE THE EARS

Blanket-stitch
EAR (RS)

STEP 7. JOIN HEAD, ARMS, AND LEGS TO THE BODY

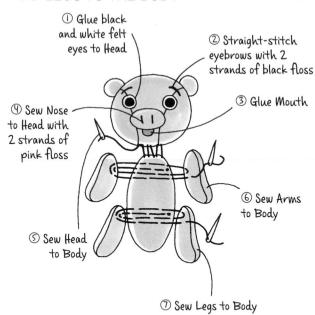

① Glue black and white felt eyes to Head

② Straight-stitch eyebrows with 2 strands of black floss

③ Glue Mouth

④ Sew Nose to Head with 2 strands of pink floss

⑥ Sew Arms to Body

⑤ Sew Head to Body

⑦ Sew Legs to Body

STEP 8. FINISHING

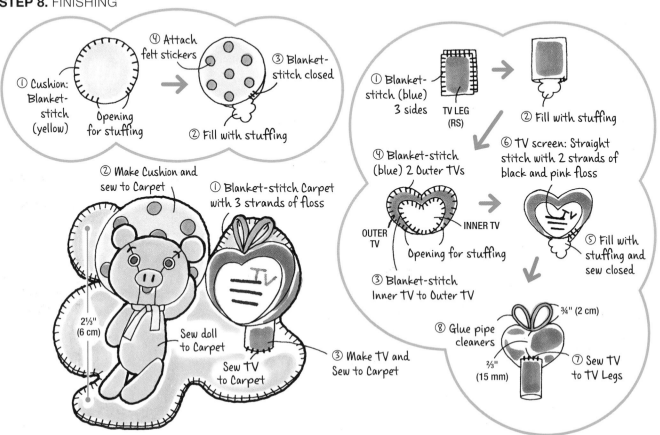

① Cushion: Blanket-stitch (yellow)

Opening for stuffing

④ Attach felt stickers

② Fill with stuffing

③ Blanket-stitch closed

② Make Cushion and sew to Carpet

① Blanket-stitch Carpet with 3 strands of floss

2⅓" (6 cm)

Sew doll to Carpet

Sew TV to Carpet

③ Make TV and Sew to Carpet

① Blanket-stitch (blue) 3 sides

TV LEG (RS)

② Fill with stuffing

④ Blanket-stitch (blue) 2 Outer TVs

OUTER TV

INNER TV

Opening for stuffing

③ Blanket-stitch Inner TV to Outer TV

⑥ TV screen: Straight stitch with 2 strands of black and pink floss

⑤ Fill with stuffing and sew closed

⑧ Glue pipe cleaners

¾" (2 cm)

⅔" (15 mm)

⑦ Sew TV to TV Legs

Pattern on page 133

MATERIALS

- 12 × 8 inches (30 × 20 cm) light brown terrycloth
- 2 × 2 inches (5 × 5 cm) white terrycloth, Fabric A
- 8 × 2 inches (20 × 5 cm) cotton jersey, Fabric B
- Scrap of tan felt
- 10 inches (25 cm) black nylon string
- Embroidery floss, dark brown and tan
- Pellets
- Stuffing
- Craft glue

STEP 1. JOIN FACE AND CHIN

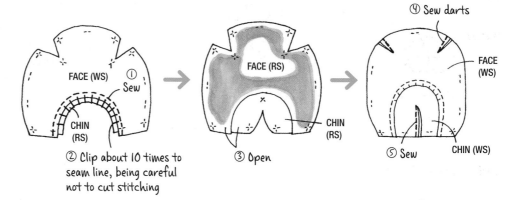

FACE (WS) ① Sew
CHIN (RS)
② Clip about 10 times to seam line, being careful not to cut stitching

FACE (RS)
CHIN (RS)
③ Open

④ Sew darts
FACE (WS)
CHIN (WS)
⑤ Sew

STEP 2. MAKE THE EAR

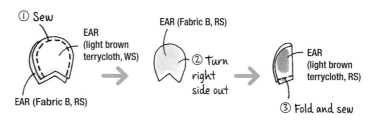

① Sew
EAR (light brown terrycloth, WS)
EAR (Fabric B, RS)

EAR (Fabric B, RS)
② Turn right side out

EAR (light brown terrycloth, RS)
③ Fold and sew

STEP 3. MAKE THE LEGS

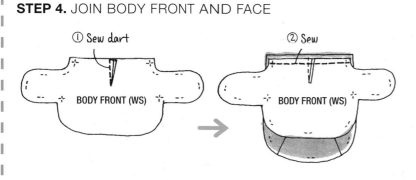

① Clip
② Sew
LEG (WS)

③ Turn right side out
LEG (RS)

④ Fill with stuffing and sew closed
Pull threads tight to create shape

⑤ Embroider toes with 2 strands of tan floss

STEP 4. JOIN BODY FRONT AND FACE

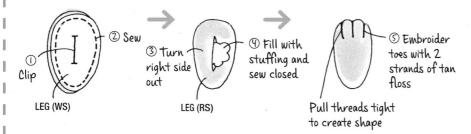

① Sew dart
BODY FRONT (WS)

② Sew
BODY FRONT (WS)

STEP 5. MAKE THE BODY BACK

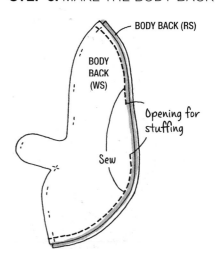

BODY BACK (RS)
BODY BACK (WS)
Opening for stuffing
Sew

STEP 6. INSERT EARS AND JOIN BODY FRONT AND BACK

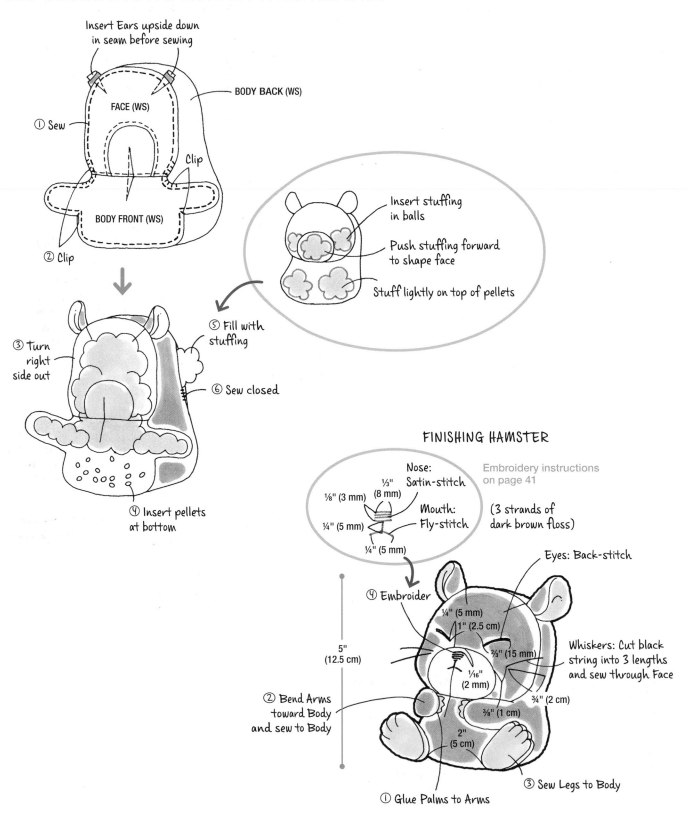

Insert Ears upside down in seam before sewing

FACE (WS)

BODY BACK (WS)

① Sew

Clip

② Clip

BODY FRONT (WS)

Insert stuffing in balls

Push stuffing forward to shape face

Stuff lightly on top of pellets

⑤ Fill with stuffing

③ Turn right side out

⑥ Sew closed

④ Insert pellets at bottom

FINISHING HAMSTER

Nose: Satin-stitch

Mouth: Fly-stitch

⅓" (8 mm)

⅛" (3 mm)

¼" (5 mm)

¼" (5 mm)

Embroidery instructions on page 41

(3 strands of dark brown floss)

④ Embroider

Eyes: Back-stitch

¼" (5 mm)

1" (2.5 cm)

⅔" (15 mm)

1⁄16" (2 mm)

Whiskers: Cut black string into 3 lengths and sew through Face

¾" (2 cm)

⅜" (1 cm)

5" (12.5 cm)

② Bend Arms toward Body and sew to Body

2" (5 cm)

① Glue Palms to Arms

③ Sew Legs to Body

Instructions for 35 Piglet, page 27

Pattern on page 131

Instruction is similar to #37

MATERIALS

- 12 × 8 inches (30 × 20 cm) pink terrycloth, Fabric A
- 6 × 2 inches (15 × 5 cm) beige cotton jersey, Fabric B
- Scrap of beige felt
- 2 inches (5 cm) elastic string
- Embroidery floss, dark brown and pink
- Pellets
- Stuffing
- Craft glue

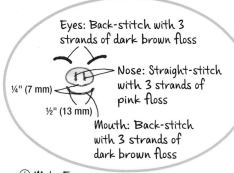

Eyes: Back-stitch with 3 strands of dark brown floss

Nose: Straight-stitch with 3 strands of pink floss

¼" (7 mm)

½" (13 mm)

Mouth: Back-stitch with 3 strands of dark brown floss

⑧ Bend Ears forward and sew to Face

① Make Ears (Hamster step 2)

1½" (4 cm)

⑨ Attach Nose to Face

⑥ Insert Ears and Tail, sew Front and Back together

④ Sew Body Front and Face together (Hamster step 4)

③ Make Paws: Sew Paws with right sides together, leaving opening; turn right side out, sew opening closed. Sew to arms.

1" (2.5 cm)

⅜" (1 cm)

Fabric B

4¾" (12 cm)

2" (5 cm)

2" (5 cm)

⑦ Make Legs (Hamster step 3) and sew to Body Front

⑤ Make Body Back (Hamster step 5)

¼" (5 mm)

② Tail: Knot elastic string and sew to tail location, hiding knot within body.

Make a knot at the end of tail

Instructions for 36 Baby Seal, page 27

Pattern on page 132

Instruction is similar to #37

MATERIALS

- 12 × 8 inches (30 × 20 cm) white terrycloth, Fabric A
- 2 × 2 inches (5 × 5 cm) gray terrycloth, Fabric B
- Two ⅛-inch (3 mm) buttons for eyes
- Black embroidery floss
- Pellets
- Stuffing

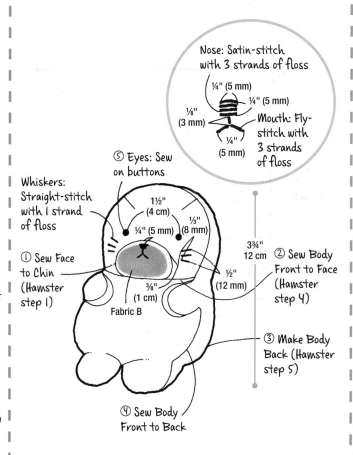

Nose: Satin-stitch with 3 strands of floss

¼" (5 mm)

⅛" (3 mm)

¼" (5 mm)

Mouth: Fly-stitch with 3 strands of floss

¼" (5 mm)

⑤ Eyes: Sew on buttons

Whiskers: Straight-stitch with 1 strand of floss

1½" (4 cm)

¼" (5 mm)

⅓" (8 mm)

① Sew Face to Chin (Hamster step 1)

⅜" (1 cm)

Fabric B

3¾" 12 cm

② Sew Body Front to Face (Hamster step 4)

½" (12 mm)

③ Make Body Back (Hamster step 5)

④ Sew Body Front to Back

Instructions for 38 Panda,
page 27

Pattern on page 134

Instruction is similar to #37

MATERIALS

- 12 × 6 inches (30 × 15 cm) white terrycloth, Fabric A
- 10 × 4 inches (25 × 10 cm) black terrycloth, Fabric B
- Scrap of black felt
- Two ⅛-inch (4 mm) buttons for eyes
- Black embroidery floss
- Pellets
- Stuffing
- Craft glue

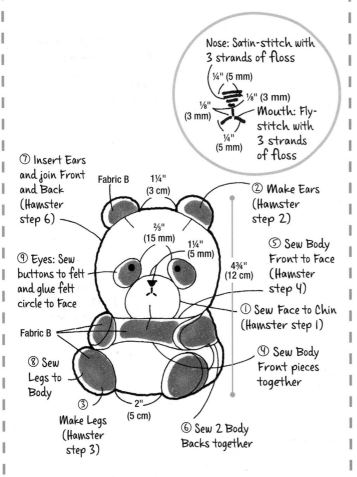

Nose: Satin-stitch with 3 strands of floss

¼" (5 mm)

⅛" (3 mm)

⅛" (3 mm)

Mouth: Fly-stitch with 3 strands of floss

¼" (5 mm)

⑦ Insert Ears and join Front and Back (Hamster step 6)

Fabric B

1¼" (3 cm)

② Make Ears (Hamster step 2)

⑨ Eyes: Sew buttons to felt and glue felt circle to Face

⅔" (15 mm)

1¼" (5 mm)

4¾" (12 cm)

⑤ Sew Body Front to Face (Hamster step 4)

① Sew Face to Chin (Hamster step 1)

Fabric B

⑧ Sew Legs to Body

④ Sew Body Front pieces together

③ Make Legs (Hamster step 3)

2" (5 cm)

⑥ Sew 2 Body Backs together

Instructions for 39 Frog,
page 27

Pattern on page 135

Instruction is similar to #37

MATERIALS

- 12 × 8 inches (30 × 20 cm) green terrycloth, Fabric A
- 8 × 4 inches (20 × 10 cm) white terrycloth, Fabric B
- Two ⅛-inch (4 mm) buttons for eyes
- Dark brown embroidery floss
- Pellets
- Stuffing

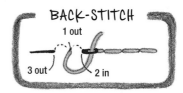

BACK-STITCH

1 out

3 out

2 in

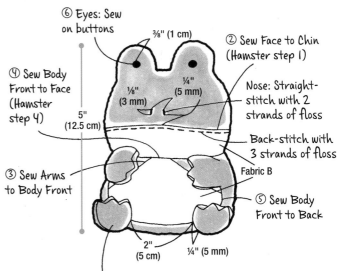

⑥ Eyes: Sew on buttons

⅜" (1 cm)

② Sew Face to Chin (Hamster step 1)

④ Sew Body Front to Face (Hamster step 4)

⅛" (3 mm)

¼" (5 mm)

Nose: Straight-stitch with 2 strands of floss

5" (12.5 cm)

Back-stitch with 3 strands of floss

Fabric B

③ Sew Arms to Body Front

⑤ Sew Body Front to Back

2" (5 cm)

¼" (5 mm)

① Make Feet: Sew Feet with right sides together, leaving opening; turn right side out, sew opening closed; sew to Legs

Instructions for 40 Kiki, 41 Hana, 42 Nick, pages 28–29

Pattern on page 136

MATERIALS (FOR ONE)

- 8 × 10 inches (20 × 25 cm) cotton for body
- 6 × 2 inches (15 × 5 cm) cotton for pants, Fabric A
- 8 × 12 inches (20 × 30 cm) cotton for hair, Fabric B
- Two ¼-inch (6 mm) two-hole buttons for eyes
- Stuffing
- Acrylic paint
- Craft glue

41 Hana

42 Nick

STEP 1. MAKE THE HEAD

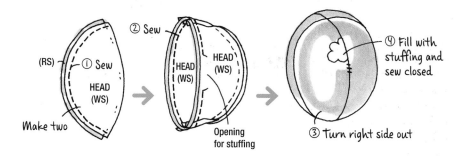

(RS)

① Sew

HEAD (WS)

Make two

② Sew

HEAD (WS)

HEAD (WS)

Opening for stuffing

④ Fill with stuffing and sew closed

③ Turn right side out

STEP 2. MAKE THE BODY

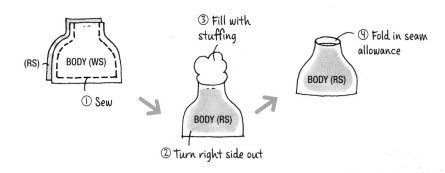

(RS)

BODY (WS)

① Sew

③ Fill with stuffing

BODY (RS)

② Turn right side out

④ Fold in seam allowance

BODY (RS)

STEP 3. MAKE THE ARMS

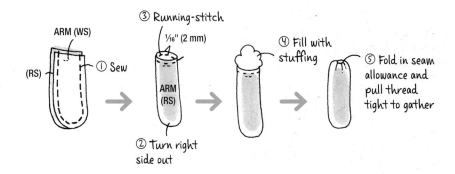

ARM (WS)

(RS)

① Sew

③ Running-stitch

1/16" (2 mm)

ARM (RS)

② Turn right side out

④ Fill with stuffing

⑤ Fold in seam allowance and pull thread tight to gather

STEP 4. MAKE THE LEGS

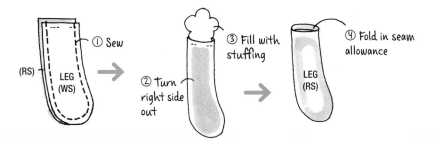

(RS)

LEG (WS)

① Sew

② Turn right side out

③ Fill with stuffing

④ Fold in seam allowance

LEG (RS)

STEP 5. JOIN HEAD, LEGS, AND ARMS TO BODY

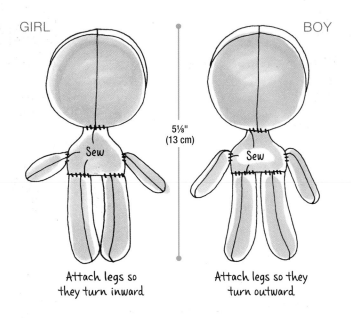

GIRL

BOY

5⅛"
(13 cm)

Sew

Sew

Attach legs so
they turn inward

Attach legs so they
turn outward

STEP 6. MAKE PANTS AND ATTACH TO BODY

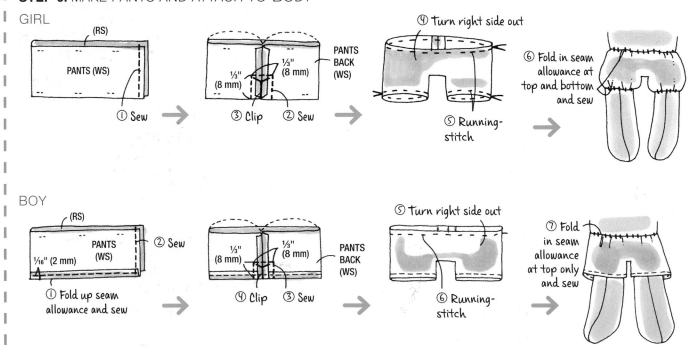

GIRL

(RS)

PANTS (WS)

① Sew

⅓"
(8 mm)

⅓"
(8 mm)

PANTS
BACK
(WS)

③ Clip   ② Sew

④ Turn right side out

⑤ Running-
stitch

⑥ Fold in seam
allowance at
top and bottom
and sew

BOY

(RS)

PANTS
(WS)

② Sew

1⁄16" (2 mm)

① Fold up seam
allowance and sew

⅓"
(8 mm)

⅓"
(8 mm)

PANTS
BACK
(WS)

④ Clip   ③ Sew

⑤ Turn right side out

⑥ Running-
stitch

⑦ Fold
in seam
allowance
at top only
and sew

STEP 7. MAKE THE FACE

GIRL & BOY

Paint on brown freckles, black eye lashes, and red mouth

½" (13 mm)

Eyes: Sew on buttons

1¼" (3 cm)

Cheeks

STEP 8. MAKE THE HAIR

KIKI

Make 15 sections of Hair according to diagram

SIDE
6¼" (16 cm)
Fabric B
⅜" (1 cm)
Sew
⅓" (7 mm)

FRONT and BACK
3½" (9 cm)
1¼" (3 cm)
FRONT
Wind 15 times
Fabric B
⅜" (1 cm)
Sew
⅓" (7 mm)

Glue Hair to Head

SIDE HAIR
FRONT
BACK

Glue Front and Back Hair to Head

FRONT
FRONT
BACK
BACK

Glue Hair to Head

Cut bangs

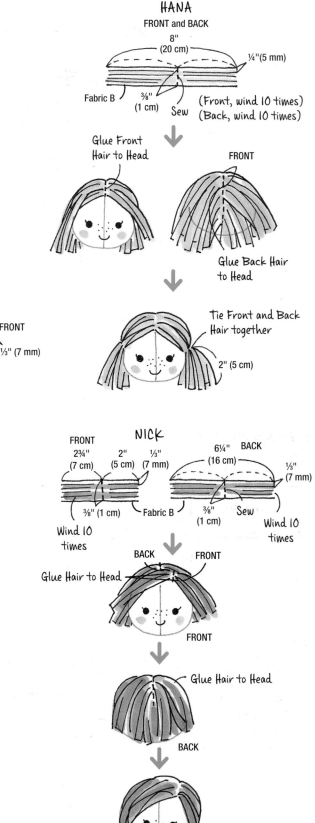

HANA

FRONT and BACK
8" (20 cm)
¼" (5 mm)
Fabric B
⅜" (1 cm)
Sew
(Front, wind 10 times)
(Back, wind 10 times)

Glue Front Hair to Head

FRONT

Glue Back Hair to Head

Tie Front and Back Hair together

2" (5 cm)

NICK

FRONT
2¾" (7 cm)
2" (5 cm)
⅓" (7 mm)
6¼" (16 cm)
BACK
⅓" (7 mm)
⅜" (1 cm)
Fabric B
⅜" (1 cm)
Sew
Wind 10 times
Wind 10 times

BACK
FRONT
Glue Hair to Head

FRONT

Glue Hair to Head

BACK

Cut to short haircut

Instructions for 40a Kiki, page 29

Pattern on page 136

MATERIALS FOR ONE-PIECE DRESS
- 6 × 8 inches (15 × 20 cm) cotton flower print, Fabric A
- 2 × 2 inches (5 × 5 cm) red faux leather, Fabric B
- Two ¼-inch (6 mm) two-hole buttons
- Two pairs of snaps

FOR HAT
- 12 × 6 inches (30 × 15 cm) white denim
- 8 × 2 inches (20 × 5 cm) fusible interfacing
- Two ¼-inch (6 mm) two-hole buttons

STEP 1. SEW SHOULDER OF DRESS

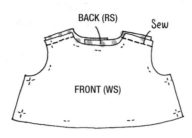

BACK (RS)   Sew
FRONT (WS)

STEP 2. SEW ARMHOLE

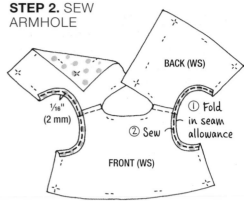

BACK (WS)
① Fold in seam allowance
② Sew
1/16" (2 mm)
FRONT (WS)

STEP 3. SEW NECKLINE

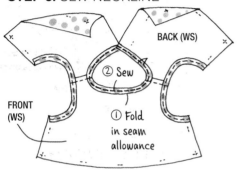

BACK (WS)
② Sew
FRONT (WS)
① Fold in seam allowance

STEP 4. SEW SIDE SEAMS

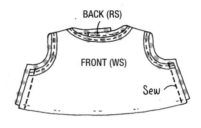

BACK (RS)
FRONT (WS)
Sew

STEP 5. SEW HEM

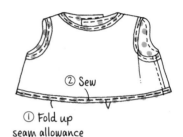

② Sew
① Fold up seam allowance

STEP 6. FINISH EDGE OF BACK

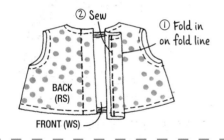

② Sew
① Fold in on fold line
BACK (RS)
FRONT (WS)

STEP 7. ATTACH SNAPS

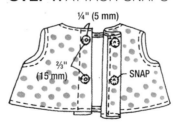

¼" (5 mm)
2/3" (15 mm)
SNAP

STEP 8. ATTACH COLLAR

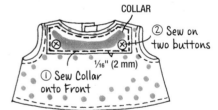

COLLAR
② Sew on two buttons
1/16" (2 mm)
① Sew Collar onto Front

STEP 1. SEW HAT CROWN

HAT CROWN (WS)
① Sew
(RS)
CROWN (RS)
② Sew 6 pieces together

STEP 2. SEW HAT BRIM

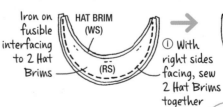

Iron on fusible interfacing to 2 Hat Brims
HAT BRIM (WS)
(RS)
① With right sides facing, sew 2 Hat Brims together
② turn right side out
③ Stitch edge
1/16" (2 mm)

STEP 3. ATTACH HAT BRIM

HAT BRIM
Sew
HAT CROWN (RS)

STEP 4. SEW HAT EDGE

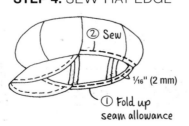

② Sew
1/16" (2 mm)
① Fold up seam allowance

STEP 5. ATTACH HAT BAND

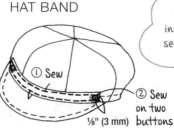

① Sew
② Sew on two buttons
1/8" (3 mm)

For Boot instructions, see next page

MATERIALS FOR DRESS

- 6 × 4 inches (15 × 10 cm) cotton flower print, Fabric A
- 4 × 2 inches (10 × 5 cm) white faux leather, Fabric B
- Two ¼-inch (6 mm) two-hole buttons
- Two pairs of snaps

FOR BAG

- 2 × 4 inches (5 × 10 cm) white fur
- One ⅜-inch (9 mm) flower-shaped button
- 4 inches (10 cm) thin cord

FOR 40A AND 40B BOOTS

- 6 × 2 inches (15 × 5 cm) faux red leather

BOOTS
(SAME FOR 41 AND 42)

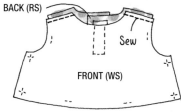

STEP 3. SEW ARMHOLES

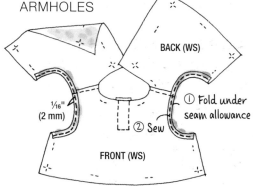

STEP 1. ATTACH FRONT PANEL TO FRONT

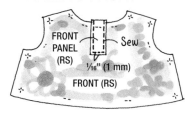

STEP 2. SEW SHOULDERS

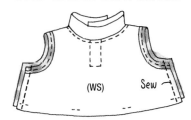

STEP 4. ATTACH COLLAR

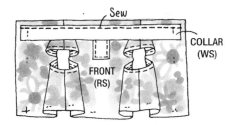

STEP 5. SEW SIDE SEAMS

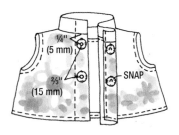

STEP 6. SEW HEM

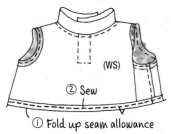

STEP 7. FINISH EDGE OF BACK

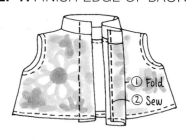

STEP 8. ATTACH SNAPS

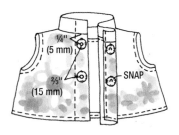

STEP 9. SEW BUTTONS TO FRONT PANEL

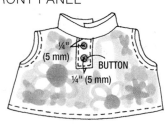

STEP 10. MAKE BAG

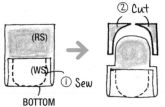
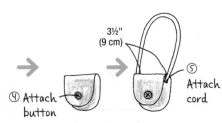

Pattern for Bag
Seam allowances included

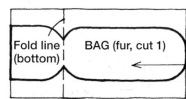

MATERIALS FOR DRESS
- 6 × 4 inches (15 × 10 cm) striped cotton, Fabric A
- 4 × 1 inches (10 × 2 cm) polka-dotted cotton, Fabric B
- Two pairs of snaps

FOR BOOTS
- 6 × 2 inches (15 × 5 cm) white faux leather
- Two ⅕-inch (5 mm) two-hole buttons

FOR HAT
- Small quantities of yellow and white yarn
- One ½-inch (13 mm) pom-pom

STEPS FOR 1–7 ARE SAME AS 41B (PAGE 91)

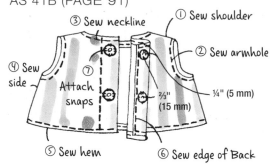

③ Sew neckline
① Sew shoulder
② Sew armhole
④ Sew side
⑦ Attach snaps
⅔" (15 mm)
¼" (5 mm)
⑤ Sew hem
⑥ Sew edge of Back

STEP 8. GATHER FABRIC AROUND ARMHOLE

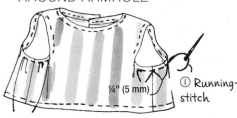

① Running-stitch
¼" (5 mm)
② Pull thread to gather

STEP 9. MAKE SCARF

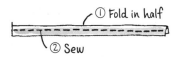

① Fold in half
② Sew

STEP 10. MAKE HAT

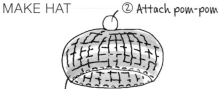

② Attach pom-pom
① Crocheted Hat (See crochet chart)

Instructions for Crocheted Hat

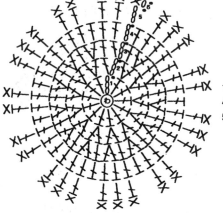

1–3 rows yellow
4 rows white
5–6 rows yellow

CAST ON

NARROW STITCH

① Loop end of yarn twice around left index finger

② Pass hook through the loop and draw yarn back through

③ Repeat for as many stitches as needed on each row

 CHAIN STITCH

① ② ③ ④ ⑤ ⑥
One stitch

Initial loop on hook does not count as one stitch

 DRAWING STITCH

① Pass hook in the direction of arrow

② Draw yarn back one stitch at one time

 LONG STITCH

① Draw hook and yarn back in the direction of arrow

Insert hook in the third chain stitch from hook

BASE STITCH

② Draw hook through two loops

③ ④

LONG STITCH – MAKE STITCH

① Make a long single stitch

② Pass hook in the same stitch again

③

Instructions for 41b Hana, page 29

Pattern on page 137

MATERIALS FOR DRESS
- 6 × 4 inches (15 × 10 cm) cotton print
- Two pairs of snaps

FOR BAG
- 2 × 2 inches (5 × 5 cm) dark brown faux leather, Fabric A
- 2 × 2 inches (5 × 5 cm) printed faux leather, Fabric B
- 4 inches (10 cm) thin cord

FOR BOOTS
- 6 × 2 inches (15 × 5 cm) white faux leather
- Two ¼-inch (6 mm) two-hole buttons

STEP 1. SEW HEM OF DRESS FRONT

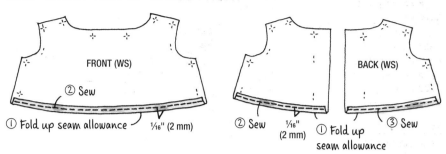

FRONT (WS)
② Sew
① Fold up seam allowance
1⁄16" (2 mm)

BACK (WS)
② Sew
1⁄16" (2 mm)
① Fold up seam allowance
③ Sew

STEP 2. SEW FRONT PLEAT

(WS)
① Sew with wrong sides together
FRONT (RS)
1⁄16" (2 mm)

③ Fold
¼" (5 mm)
② Adjust folded lines in the center
④ Sew

STEP 3. SEW SHOULDERS

BACK (RS)
Sew
FRONT (WS)

STEP 4. SEW ARMHOLES

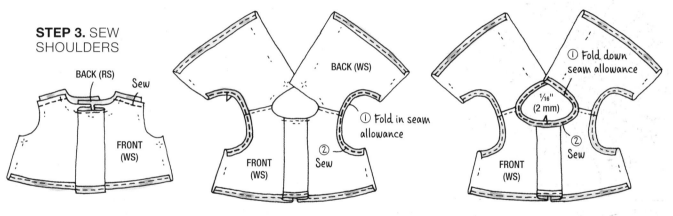

BACK (WS)
① Fold in seam allowance
FRONT (WS)
② Sew

STEP 5. SEW NECKLINE

① Fold down seam allowance
1⁄16" (2 mm)
FRONT (WS)
② Sew

STEP 6. SEW SIDE SEAMS

BACK (RS)
FRONT (WS)
Sew

STEP 7. FINISH EDGE OF BACK

① Fold
BACK (RS)
② Sew

STEP 8. ATTACH SNAPS

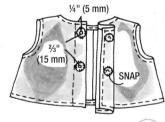

¼" (5 mm)
2⁄3" (15 mm)
SNAP

STEP 9. MAKE BAG

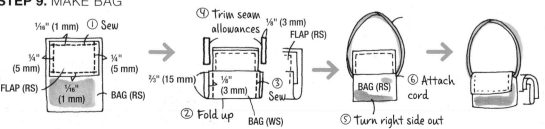

1⁄16" (1 mm)
① Sew
¼" (5 mm)
¼" (5 mm)
FLAP (RS)
1⁄16" (1 mm)
BAG (RS)

④ Trim seam allowances
1⁄8" (3 mm)
FLAP (RS)
2⁄3" (15 mm)
1⁄8" (3 mm)
③ Sew
② Fold up
BAG (WS)

FLAP (RS)
BAG (RS)
⑥ Attach cord
⑤ Turn right side out

Instructions for Boots are on page 89

MATERIALS
FOR SHIRT
- 8 × 6 inches (20 × 15 cm) striped cotton
- Two pairs of snaps

FOR PANTS
- 4 × 6 inches (10 × 15 cm) black cotton

FOR HAT
- 6 × 8 inches (15 × 20 cm) striped twill
- 6 × 2 inches (15 × 5 cm) fusible interfacing

SHIRT

STEP 1. SEW SHOULDERS

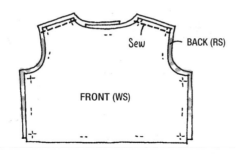

STEP 2. ATTACH COLLAR

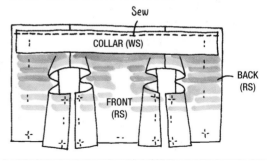

STEP 3. SEW HEM OF SLEEVE AND ATTACH

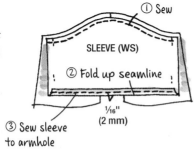

STEP 4. SEW SIDE SEAM OF SHIRT AND SLEEVE

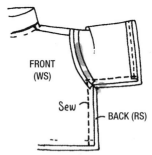

STEP 5. SEW SHIRT HEM

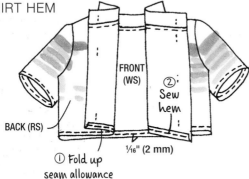

STEP 6. FINISH EDGE OF BACK

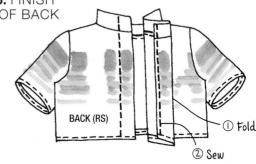

STEP 7. ATTACH SNAPS

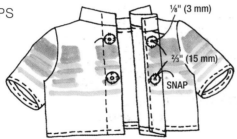

PANTS

STEP 1. SEW WAIST AND HEM

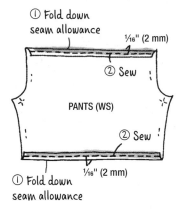

① Fold down seam allowance

1⁄16" (2 mm)

② Sew

PANTS (WS)

② Sew

1⁄16" (2 mm)

① Fold down seam allowance

STEP 2. SEW CENTER SEAM AND HEM

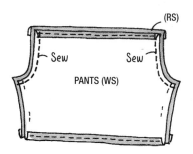

(RS)

Sew

Sew

PANTS (WS)

STEP 3. SEW INSEAM

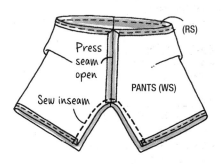

(RS)

Press seam open

Sew inseam

PANTS (WS)

HAT

STEP 1. SEW DART

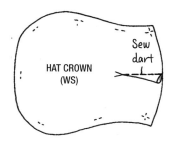

HAT CROWN (WS)

Sew dart

STEP 2. ATTACH CROWN SIDE

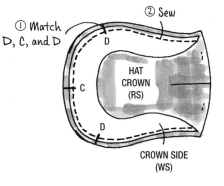

① Match D, C, and D

② Sew

D

C

HAT CROWN (RS)

D

CROWN SIDE (WS)

STEP 3. MAKE HAT BRIM

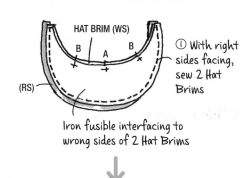

HAT BRIM (WS)

B   A   B

(RS)

① With right sides facing, sew 2 Hat Brims

Iron fusible interfacing to wrong sides of 2 Hat Brims

② Turn right side out

③ Stitch

HAT BRIM (RS)

1⁄16" (2 mm)

STEP 4. ATTACH HAT BRIM

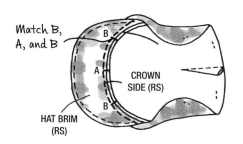

Match B, A, and B

B

A

CROWN SIDE (RS)

B

HAT BRIM (RS)

STEP 5. SEW EDGE

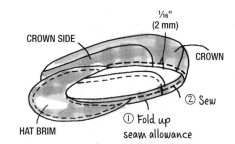

1⁄16" (2 mm)

CROWN SIDE

CROWN

② Sew

① Fold up seam allowance

HAT BRIM

Pattern on page 137

MATERIALS
FOR SHIRT
- 8 × 4 inches (20 × 10 cm) cotton print
- Two pairs of snaps

FOR PANTS
- 6 × 4 inches (15 × 10 cm) checked flannel, Fabric A
- 4 × 8 inches (10 × 20 cm) dark brown faux leather, Fabric B
- Two ¼-inch (6 mm) two-hole buttons

FOR HAT
- 6 × 8 inches (15 × 20 cm) striped twill

STEP 1. SEW SHOULDER AND NECKLINE

② Fold in seam allowance
BACK (WS)
① Sew shoulder seam
FRONT (WS)
③ Sew

STEPS 2–6 ARE THE SAME AS STEPS 3–7 OF 42A (PAGE 92)

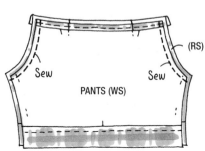

⑥ Attach snaps
② Hem sleeves and attach
③ Sew side seam of shirt and sleeve
④ Sew hem
⑤ Fold and sew

STEP 1. SEW TACKS

② Fold to the center
① Sew
PANTS (WS)

STEP 2. ATTACH CUFFS

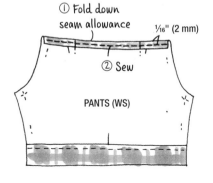

PANTS CUFFS (WS)   ② Sew
FRONT   BACK
RIGHT PANTS (RS)
① Fold toward front
(RS)

PANTS CUFFS (WS)
BACK   FRONT
① Fold toward front
(RS)
LEFT PANTS (RS)

STEP 3. FOLD AND SEW PANTS CUFFS

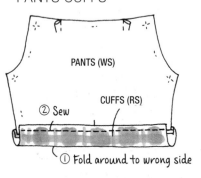

PANTS (WS)
② Sew
CUFFS (RS)
① Fold around to wrong side

STEP 4. SEW WAISTLINE

① Fold down seam allowance
1/16" (2 mm)
② Sew
PANTS (WS)

STEP 5. SEW CENTER SEAMS

(RS)
Sew   Sew
PANTS (WS)

STEP 6. SEW INSEAM

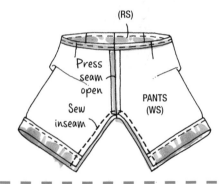

(RS)
Press seam open
Sew inseam
PANTS (WS)

STEP 7. ATTACH SUSPENDERS AND BUTTONS

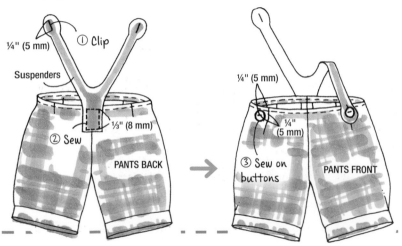

① Clip
¼" (5 mm)
Suspenders
② Sew
1/3" (8 mm)
PANTS BACK

¼" (5 mm)
¼" (5 mm)
③ Sew on buttons
PANTS FRONT

Instructions for 43, 44, 45 Cuties, pages 30–31

Pattern on page 138

MATERIALS FOR BODY

- 8 × 6 inches (20 × 15 cm) beige cotton, Fabric A
- 4 × 2 inches (10 × 5 cm) white cotton, Fabric B
- 76 yards (70 m) thin yarn]
- Stuffing
- Acrylic paint

STEP 1. MAKE THE BODY

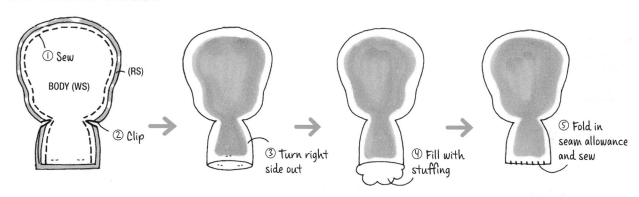

① Sew

BODY (WS)

(RS)

② Clip

③ Turn right side out

④ Fill with stuffing

⑤ Fold in seam allowance and sew

STEP 2. MAKE THE ARMS

⑤ Fold in seam allowance

(RS)

ARM (WS)

① Sew

② Clip

③ Turn right side out

④ Fill with stuffing

STEP 4. JOIN ARMS AND LEGS TO BODY

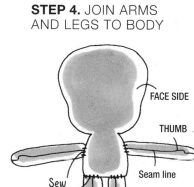

FACE SIDE

THUMB

Sew

Seam line

STEP 3. MAKE THE LEGS

④ Fold in seam allowance

(RS)

LEG (WS)

① Sew

② Turn right side out

③ Fill with stuffing

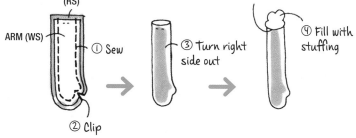

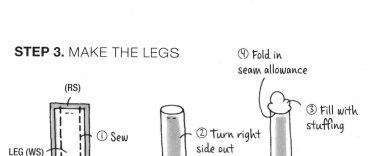

STEP 5. MAKE THE PANTS

① Fold in seam allowances at top and bottom; sew bottom only

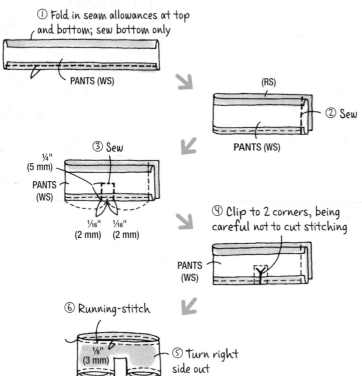

PANTS (WS)

(RS)
② Sew
PANTS (WS)

③ Sew
¼" (5 mm)
PANTS (WS)
¹⁄₁₆" (2 mm) ¹⁄₁₆" (2 mm)

④ Clip to 2 corners, being careful not to cut stitching
PANTS (WS)

⑥ Running-stitch

⅛" (3 mm)
⑤ Turn right side out

STEP 6. ATTACH PANTS

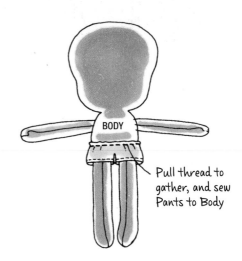

BODY

Pull thread to gather, and sew Pants to Body

STEP 7. MAKE THE HAIR (43, 44, 45)

Cut the yarn into 50 strands of equal length. Stack them together and fold in half.

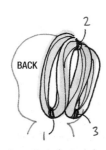

Twist to form point

Hold folded end of thread ends in left hand

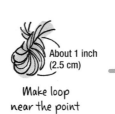

About 1 inch (2.5 cm)

Make loop near the point

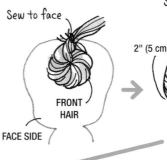

Sew to face

FRONT HAIR

FACE SIDE

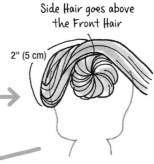

Side Hair goes above the Front Hair

2" (5 cm)

2
BACK
1
3

Sew thread strands together and sew to Head at locations 1, 2, 3

4

Sew at location 4

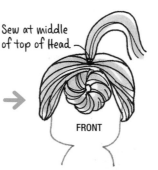

Sew at middle of top of Head

FRONT

43 FINISH HAIR

Separate Hair for right and left sides and sew top of pigtails to Head

44 FINISH HAIR

Separate into five bunches and make braids

45 FINISH HAIR

① Separate into six bunches and twist

② Sew twists to top of Head

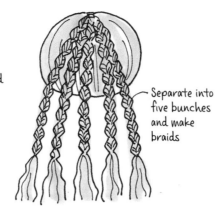

STEP 8. MAKE THE FACE

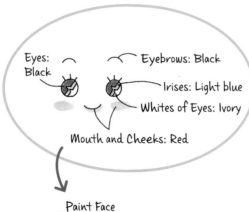

Eyes: Black

Eyebrows: Black

Irises: Light blue

Whites of Eyes: Ivory

Mouth and Cheeks: Red

Paint Face

5⅛" (13 cm)

MATERIALS FOR DOLL STAND

- 1 × 2 × ½ inch (3 × 6 × 1.5 cm) wood piece
- 7 inches (18 cm) 19-gauge wire

② Paint top in two different colors

⅛" (3 mm)

⅔" (15 mm)

⅜" (1 cm)

⅜" (1 cm)

1¼" (3 cm)

⅜" (1 cm)

2⅓" (6 cm)

① Paint sides

③ Make two holes for wire and fill with glue

3" (7.5 cm)

④ Bend wire into a loop

⑤ Insert wire in the holes

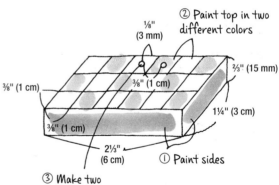

MATERIALS FOR TUNIC

- 4 × 4 inches (10 × 10 cm) cotton print
- Two ¼-inch (6 mm) two-hole buttons

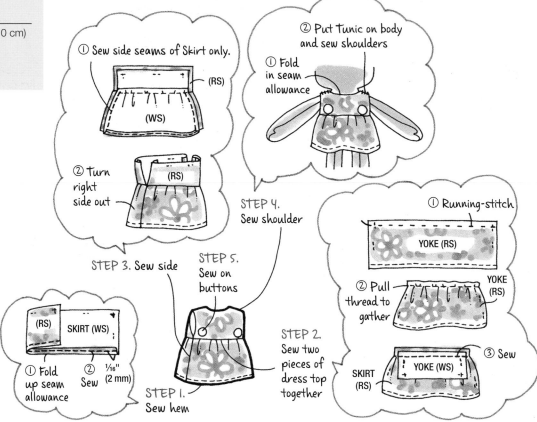

MATERIALS FOR PANTS

- 6 × 4 inches (15 × 10 cm) white faux leather

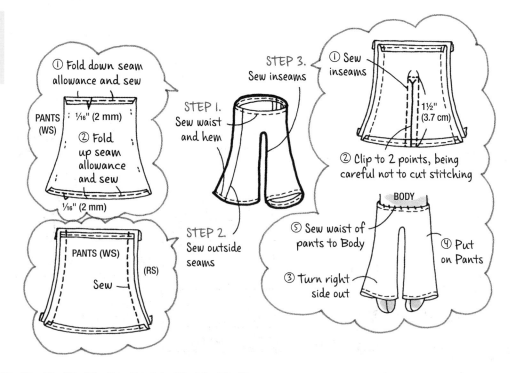

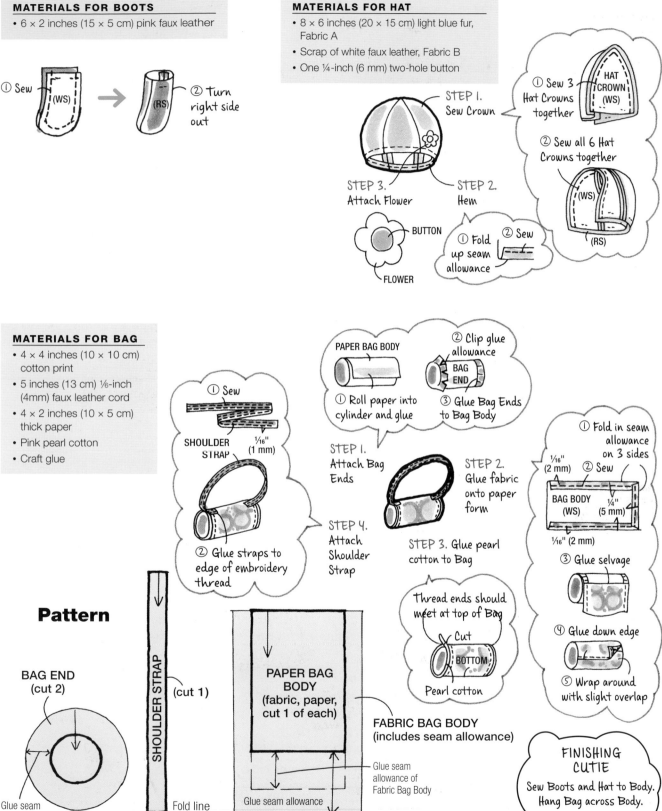

MATERIALS FOR BOOTS
• 6 × 2 inches (15 × 5 cm) pink faux leather

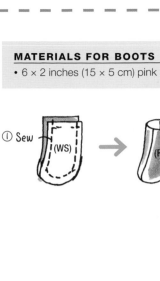

① Sew (WS)

② Turn right side out (RS)

MATERIALS FOR HAT
• 8 × 6 inches (20 × 15 cm) light blue fur, Fabric A
• Scrap of white faux leather, Fabric B
• One ¼-inch (6 mm) two-hole button

STEP 1. Sew Crown

STEP 3. Attach Flower

STEP 2. Hem

① Sew 3 Hat Crowns together

HAT CROWN (WS)

② Sew all 6 Hat Crowns together

(WS)

(RS)

① Fold up seam allowance

② Sew

BUTTON

FLOWER

MATERIALS FOR BAG
• 4 × 4 inches (10 × 10 cm) cotton print
• 5 inches (13 cm) ⅛-inch (4mm) faux leather cord
• 4 × 2 inches (10 × 5 cm) thick paper
• Pink pearl cotton
• Craft glue

① Sew

SHOULDER STRAP

1/16" (1 mm)

② Glue straps to edge of embroidery thread

PAPER BAG BODY

① Roll paper into cylinder and glue

② Clip glue allowance

BAG END

③ Glue Bag Ends to Bag Body

STEP 1. Attach Bag Ends

STEP 2. Glue fabric onto paper form

STEP 4. Attach Shoulder Strap

STEP 3. Glue pearl cotton to Bag

Thread ends should meet at top of Bag

Cut

BOTTOM

Pearl cotton

① Fold in seam allowance on 3 sides

1/16" (2 mm)

② Sew

BAG BODY (WS)

¼" (5 mm)

1/16" (2 mm)

③ Glue selvage

④ Glue down edge

⑤ Wrap around with slight overlap

Pattern

BAG END (cut 2)

Glue seam allowance

SHOULDER STRAP (cut 1)

Fold line

PAPER BAG BODY (fabric, paper, cut 1 of each)

Glue seam allowance

FABRIC BAG BODY (includes seam allowance)

Glue seam allowance of Fabric Bag Body

FINISHING CUTIE
Sew Boots and Hat to Body. Hang Bag across Body.

MATERIALS FOR DRESS

- 4 × 2 inches (10 × 5 cm) checked cotton, Fabric A
- 4 × 2 inches (10 × 5 cm) striped cotton, Fabric B
- 4 inches (10 cm) ⅝-inch (1 cm) yellow cotton for belt
- 2 inches (5 cm) 14-gauge wire or small wire circle
- Craft glue

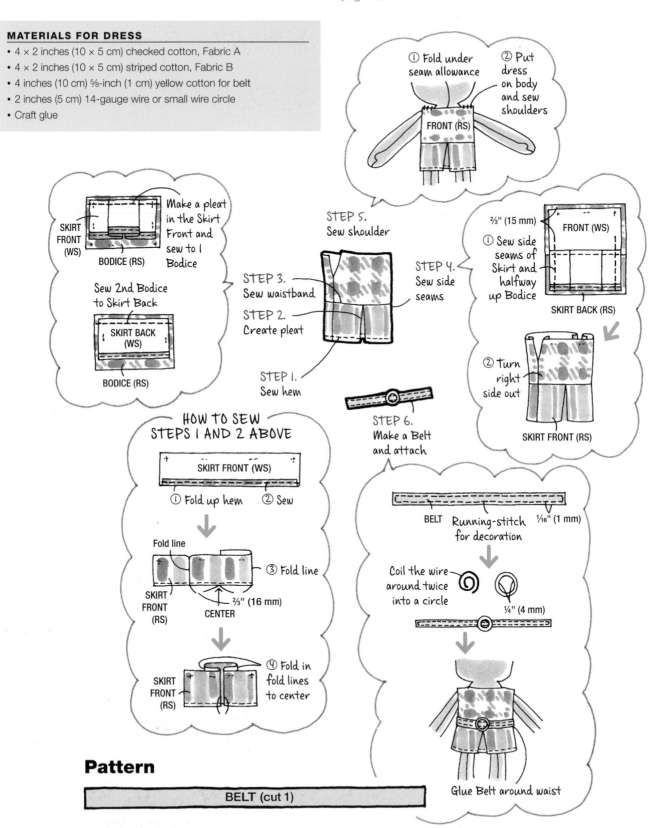

① Fold under seam allowance

② Put dress on body and sew shoulders

FRONT (RS)

Make a pleat in the Skirt Front and sew to 1 Bodice

SKIRT FRONT (WS)

BODICE (RS)

Sew 2nd Bodice to Skirt Back

SKIRT BACK (WS)

BODICE (RS)

STEP 5.
Sew shoulder

STEP 3.
Sew waistband

STEP 2.
Create pleat

STEP 1.
Sew hem

STEP 4.
Sew side seams

⅔" (15 mm)

FRONT (WS)

① Sew side seams of Skirt and halfway up Bodice

SKIRT BACK (RS)

② turn right side out

SKIRT FRONT (RS)

STEP 6.
Make a Belt and attach

HOW TO SEW STEPS 1 AND 2 ABOVE

SKIRT FRONT (WS)

① Fold up hem   ② Sew

Fold line

③ Fold line

SKIRT FRONT (RS)

CENTER   ⅔" (16 mm)

SKIRT FRONT (RS)

④ Fold in fold lines to center

BELT   Running-stitch for decoration   ¹⁄₁₆" (1 mm)

Coil the wire around twice into a circle

¼" (4 mm)

Glue Belt around waist

Pattern

BELT (cut 1)

MATERIALS FOR HEADBAND
- ¾ × 8 inches (2 × 20 cm) white faux leather
- Papier maché or fimo clay
- Acrylic paint

MATERIALS FOR BOOTS
- 6 × 2 inches (15 × 5 cm) white faux leather

- See instructions on page 99 to make the Boots

Fold in seam allowance and sew

Lace the boot
Tie a bow at the top

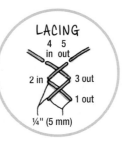

LACING
4 5
in out
2 in   3 out
1 out
¼" (5 mm)

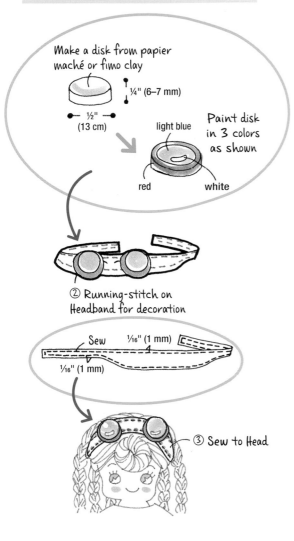

Make a disk from papier maché or fimo clay

¼" (6–7 mm)

½" (13 cm)

light blue

Paint disk in 3 colors as shown

red   white

② Running-stitch on Headband for decoration

Sew

1/16" (1 mm)

1/16" (1 mm)

③ Sew to Head

MATERIALS FOR BACKPACK
- 1 × 1 × ¼ inches (2.5 × 3.5 × 0.8 cm) wood base
- 6 × 2 inches (15 × 5 cm) pink plastic
- 4 × 2 inches (10 × 5 cm) white faux leather, Fabric A
- 2 × 2 inches (5 × 5 cm) light blue faux leather, Fabric B
- Scraps of medium yellow yarn
- Craft glue
- Sandpaper

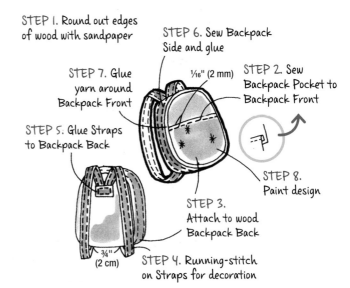

STEP 1. Round out edges of wood with sandpaper

STEP 6. Sew Backpack Side and glue

STEP 7. Glue yarn around Backpack Front

1/16" (2 mm)

STEP 2. Sew Backpack Pocket to Backpack Front

STEP 5. Glue Straps to Backpack Back

STEP 8. Paint design

STEP 3. Attach to wood Backpack Back

STEP 4. Running-stitch on Straps for decoration

¾" (2 cm)

FINISHING CUTIE

Sew Boots and Headband to Body. Hang Backpack over shoulders.

Instructions for 45 Cutie, page 32

Pattern on page 139

MATERIALS FOR DRESS

- 2 × 2 inches (5 × 5 cm) cotton check, Fabric A
- 6 × 2 inches (15 × 5 cm) black faux leather, Fabric B
- Red pearl cotton

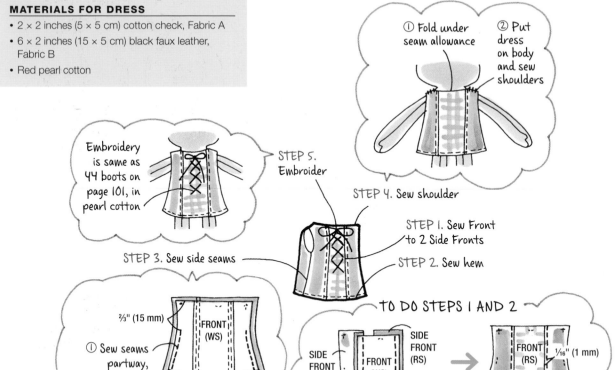

① Fold under seam allowance

② Put dress on body and sew shoulders

STEP 4. Sew shoulder

STEP 5. Embroider

STEP 1. Sew Front to 2 Side Fronts

STEP 2. Sew hem

Embroidery is same as 44 boots on page 101, in pearl cotton

STEP 3. Sew side seams

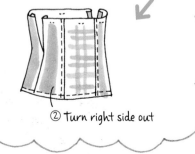

⅔" (15 mm)

FRONT (WS)

BACK (RS)

① Sew seams partway, leaving open at top for arms

② Turn right side out

TO DO STEPS 1 AND 2

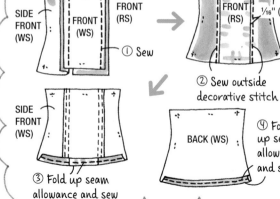

SIDE FRONT (WS)

FRONT (WS)

SIDE FRONT (RS)

① Sew

FRONT (RS)

1/16" (1 mm)

② Sew outside decorative stitch

SIDE FRONT (WS)

③ Fold up seam allowance and sew

BACK (WS)

④ Fold up seam allowance and sew

MATERIAL FOR BOOTS

- 6 × 2 inches (15 × 5 cm) faux black leather

① Sew (WS)

② Turn right side out (RS)

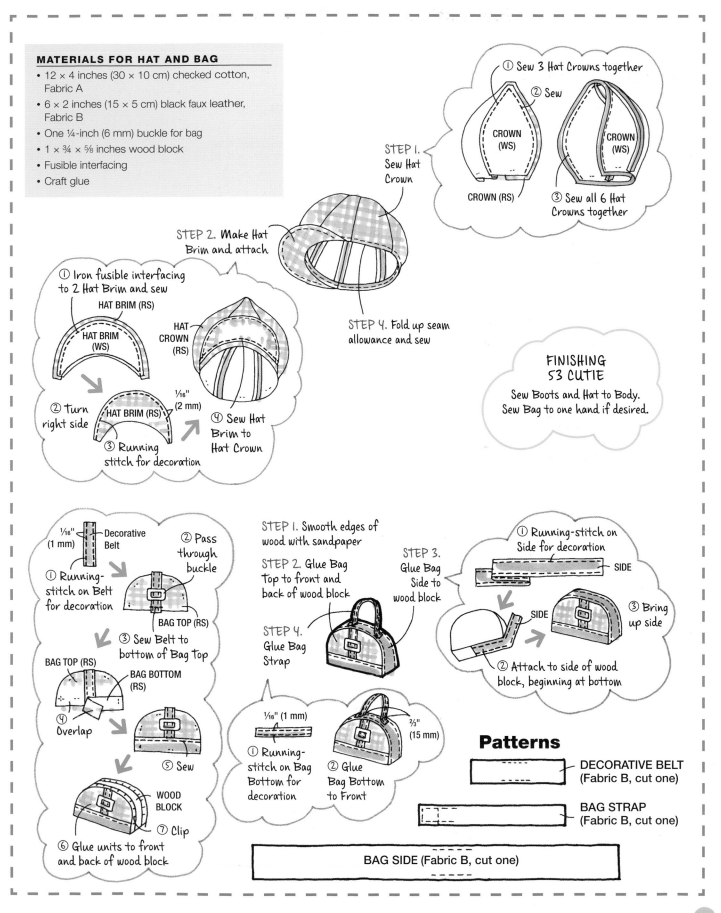

MATERIALS FOR HAT AND BAG

- 12 × 4 inches (30 × 10 cm) checked cotton, Fabric A
- 6 × 2 inches (15 × 5 cm) black faux leather, Fabric B
- One ¼-inch (6 mm) buckle for bag
- 1 × ¾ × ⅝ inches wood block
- Fusible interfacing
- Craft glue

① Sew 3 Hat Crowns together
② Sew
CROWN (WS)
CROWN (RS)
CROWN (WS)
③ Sew all 6 Hat Crowns together

STEP 1. Sew Hat Crown

STEP 2. Make Hat Brim and attach

① Iron fusible interfacing to 2 Hat Brim and sew
HAT BRIM (RS)
HAT BRIM (WS)
HAT CROWN (RS)
② turn right side
HAT BRIM (RS)
1/16" (2 mm)
③ Running stitch for decoration
④ Sew Hat Brim to Hat Crown

STEP 4. Fold up seam allowance and sew

FINISHING 53 CUTIE
Sew Boots and Hat to Body. Sew Bag to one hand if desired.

1/16" (1 mm) Decorative Belt
② Pass through buckle
① Running-stitch on Belt for decoration
BAG TOP (RS)
③ Sew Belt to bottom of Bag Top
BAG TOP (RS)
BAG BOTTOM (RS)
④ Overlap
⑤ Sew
WOOD BLOCK
⑦ Clip
⑥ Glue units to front and back of wood block

STEP 1. Smooth edges of wood with sandpaper
STEP 2. Glue Bag Top to front and back of wood block
STEP 4. Glue Bag Strap
1/16" (1 mm)
① Running-stitch on Bag Bottom for decoration
② Glue Bag Bottom to Front

STEP 3. Glue Bag Side to wood block
① Running-stitch on Side for decoration
SIDE
SIDE
③ Bring up side
② Attach to side of wood block, beginning at bottom
⅔" (15 mm)

Patterns

DECORATIVE BELT (Fabric B, cut one)

BAG STRAP (Fabric B, cut one)

BAG SIDE (Fabric B, cut one)

MATERIALS

- 8 × 4 inches (20 × 10 cm) wool
- 4 × 4 inches (10 × 10 cm) emerald green felt
- 4 × 4 inches (10 × 10 cm) bright green felt
- 2 × 2 inches (5 × 5 cm) pastel yellow felt
- Scraps of white and black felt
- Four round beads
- Four flowers
- Green yarn
- Embroidery floss, green and cream
- Stuffing
- 1¼ × 1 inch (3 × 2.5 cm) cardboard

STEP 1. MAKE THE BODY

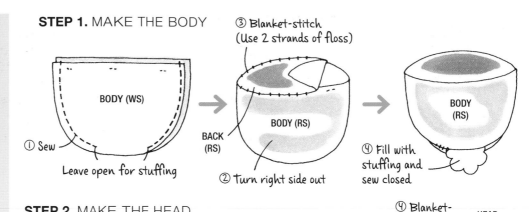

① Sew

Leave open for stuffing

BODY (WS)

③ Blanket-stitch (Use 2 strands of floss)

BACK (RS)

BODY (RS)

② Turn right side out

④ Fill with stuffing and sew closed

BODY (RS)

STEP 2. MAKE THE HEAD

HEAD CENTER (RS)

① Blanket-stitch

A

HEAD (RS)

B

② Blanket-stitch

HEAD CENTER (RS)

A

HEAD (RS)

B

④ Blanket-stitch

HEAD CENTER (RS)

HEAD (RS)

③ Fill with stuffing

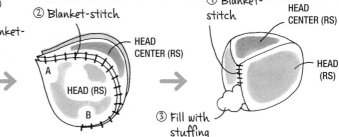

BLANKET-STITCH

FINISHING

BEAK (RS)

Blanket-stitch

BEADS

FLOWER

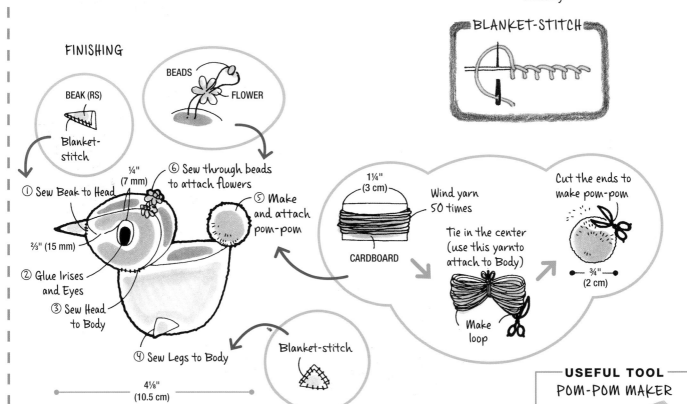

① Sew Beak to Head

¼" (7 mm)

⅔" (15 mm)

② Glue Irises and Eyes

③ Sew Head to Body

④ Sew Legs to Body

⑥ Sew through beads to attach flowers

⑤ Make and attach pom-pom

Blanket-stitch

4⅛" (10.5 cm)

1¼" (3 cm)

Wind yarn 50 times

CARDBOARD

Tie in the center (use this yarn to attach to Body)

Make loop

Cut the ends to make pom-pom

¾" (2 cm)

USEFUL TOOL
POM-POM MAKER

Make a pom-pom quickly

MATERIALS

- 16 × 8 inches (40 × 20 cm) velveteen, Fabric A
- 4 × 2 inches (10 × 5 cm) cotton print, Fabric B
- One ⅓-inch (8 mm) pom-pom
- Eight small round beads
- Two flowers
- 16 inches (40 cm) thick black yarn
- Embroidery floss, light blue
- Stuffing

STEP 1. MAKE THE BODY

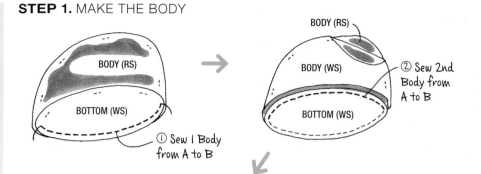

① Sew 1 Body from A to B

② Sew 2nd Body from A to B

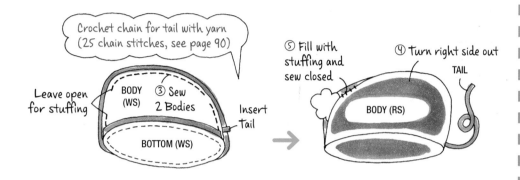

Crochet chain for tail with yarn (25 chain stitches, see page 90)

Leave open for stuffing

③ Sew 2 Bodies

Insert Tail

⑤ Fill with stuffing and sew closed

④ Turn right side out

TAIL

STEP 2. MAKE THE EAR

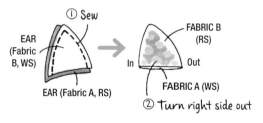

① Sew

EAR (Fabric B, WS)

EAR (Fabric A, RS)

FABRIC B (RS)

In   Out

FABRIC A (WS)

② Turn right side out

STEP 3. MAKE THE LEG

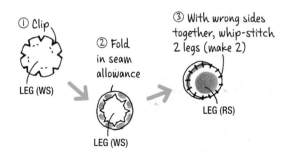

① Clip

LEG (WS)

② Fold in seam allowance

LEG (WS)

③ With wrong sides together, whip-stitch 2 legs (make 2)

LEG (RS)

STEP 4. MAKE THE ARMS

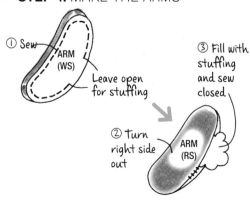

① Sew

ARM (WS)

Leave open for stuffing

③ Fill with stuffing and sew closed

② Turn right side out

ARM (RS)

STEP 5. MAKE THE HEAD

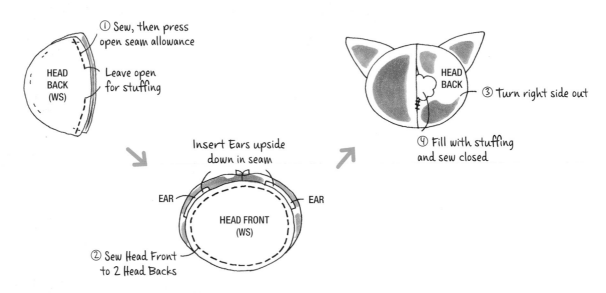

① Sew, then press open seam allowance

Leave open for stuffing

HEAD BACK (WS)

Insert Ears upside down in seam

EAR

EAR

HEAD FRONT (WS)

② Sew Head Front to 2 Head Backs

HEAD BACK

③ Turn right side out

④ Fill with stuffing and sew closed

STEP 6. FINISHING

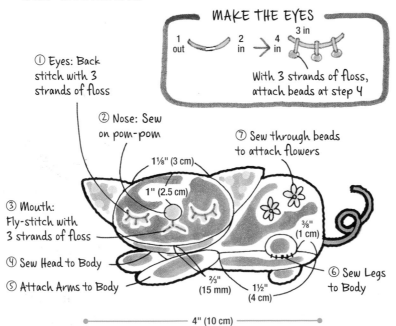

MAKE THE EYES

1 out 2 in → 4 in 3 in

With 3 strands of floss, attach beads at step 4

① Eyes: Back stitch with 3 strands of floss

② Nose: Sew on pom-pom

⑦ Sew through beads to attach flowers

1⅛" (3 cm)

1" (2.5 cm)

③ Mouth: Fly-stitch with 3 strands of floss

④ Sew Head to Body

⑤ Attach Arms to Body

⅜" (1 cm)

⅔" (15 mm)

1½" (4 cm)

⑥ Sew Legs to Body

4" (10 cm)

Instructions for 48 Dandie, pages 32–33

Pattern on page 141

MATERIALS

- 4 × 6 inches (10 × 15 cm) pink wool
- 4 × 2 inches (10 × 5 cm) pink felt
- Scrap of red felt
- Four ⅝-inch (1.2 cm) pom-poms
- Seven ½-inch (13 mm) pom-poms
- Two small round beads (eyes)
- One slightly larger round bead (nose)
- One fabric rose
- 8½ inches (20 cm) red braided trim (scarf)
- Stuffing
- Craft glue

STEP 1. MAKE THE BODY

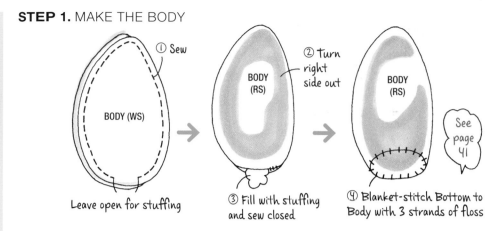

① Sew

BODY (WS)

Leave open for stuffing

② turn right side out

BODY (RS)

③ Fill with stuffing and sew closed

BODY (RS)

See page 41

④ Blanket-stitch Bottom to Body with 3 strands of floss

STEP 2. MAKE THE HEAD

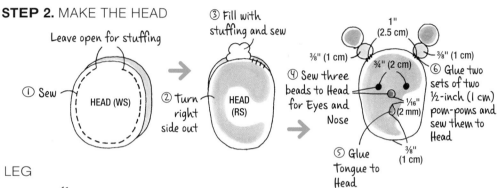

Leave open for stuffing

① Sew

HEAD (WS)

② turn right side out

③ Fill with stuffing and sew

HEAD (RS)

1" (2.5 cm)

⅜" (1 cm)

¾" (2 cm)

⅜" (1 cm)

④ Sew three beads to Head for Eyes and Nose

1/16" (2 mm)

⑥ Glue two sets of two ½-inch (1 cm) pom-poms and sew them to Head

⑤ Glue Tongue to Head

⅜" (1 cm)

STEP 3. MAKE THE LEG

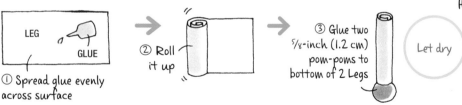

LEG   GLUE

① Spread glue evenly across surface

② Roll it up

③ Glue two ⅝-inch (1.2 cm) pom-poms to bottom of 2 Legs

Let dry

STEP 4. SEW HEAD TO BODY

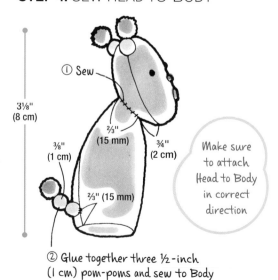

3⅛" (8 cm)

① Sew

⅔" (15 mm)

⅜" (1 cm)

¾" (2 cm)

⅔" (15 mm)

Make sure to attach Head to Body in correct direction

② Glue together three ½-inch (1 cm) pom-poms and sew to Body

STEP 5. FINISHING

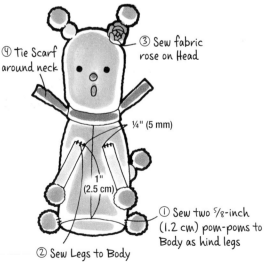

④ Tie Scarf around neck

③ Sew fabric rose on Head

¼" (5 mm)

1" (2.5 cm)

① Sew two ⅝-inch (1.2 cm) pom-poms to Body as hind legs

② Sew Legs to Body

Full pattern on page 141

MATERIALS (FOR ONE)

- 10 × 8 inches (25 × 20 cm) yellow, green, and/or pink felt
- Two 1/10-inch (3 mm) felt stickers for eyes (dark brown)
- 4 × 4 inches (10 × 10 cm) white fleece
- Two 1/4-inch (6 mm) two-hole buttons for eyes
- Two 1/5-inch (5 mm) two-hole buttons for the diapers
- Black thread for stitching
- One toy milk bottle
- 6 inches (15 cm) thin cord
- Cotton stuffing
- Acrylic paint

STEP 1. HOW TO MAKE THE HEAD

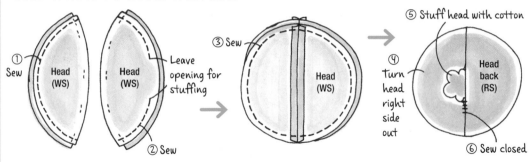

① Sew — Head (WS) — Head (WS) — Leave opening for stuffing — ② Sew — ③ Sew — Head (WS) — ④ Turn head right side out — ⑤ Stuff head with cotton — Head back (RS) — ⑥ Sew closed

STEP 2. HOW TO MAKE THE BODY

① Sew — Body (WS) — ② Turn body right side out — ③ Running-stitch — ④ Stuff with cotton — ⑤ Fold seam allowance and sew closed

STEP 3. HOW TO MAKE THE BODY

① Sew — Ear (WS) — ② Turn ear right side out — ③ Stuff ear with cotton — ④ Fold seam allowance and sew closed

STEP 4. HOW TO MAKE THE ARMS AND LEGS

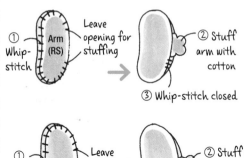

① Whip-stitch — Arm (RS) — Leave opening for stuffing — ② Stuff arm with cotton — ③ Whip-stitch closed

① Whip-stitch — Leg (RS) — Leave opening for stuffing — ② Stuff leg with cotton — ③ Whip-stitch closed

For whip-stitch instructions, see page 41

STEP 5. HOW TO ATTACH THE EYES, EYEBROWS, AND NOSE

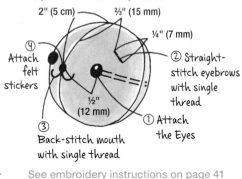

2" (5 cm) — 2/3" (15 mm) — 1/4" (7 mm) — ④ Attach felt stickers — 1/2" (12 mm) — ② Straight-stitch eyebrows with single thread — ① Attach the Eyes — ③ Back-stitch mouth with single thread

See embroidery instructions on page 41

STEP 6 PUT BODY AND HEAD TOGETHER

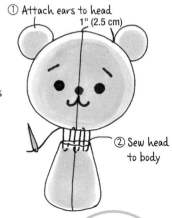

① Attach ears to head — 1" (2.5 cm) — ② Sew head to body

STEP 7 ATTACH ARMS AND LEGS

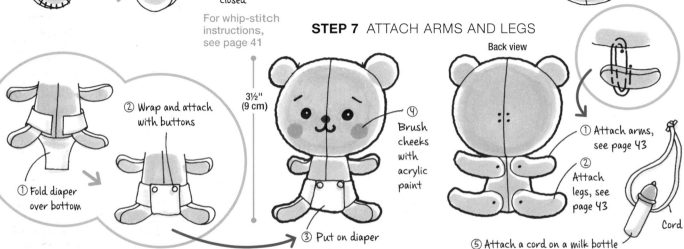

② Wrap and attach with buttons — ① Fold diaper over bottom

3½" (9 cm) — ④ Brush cheeks with acrylic paint — ③ Put on diaper

Back view — ① Attach arms, see page 43 — ② Attach legs, see page 43 — ⑤ Attach a cord on a milk bottle — Cord

Full pattern on page 142

MATERIALS FOR 52 HE-GOAT

- 12 × 8 inches (30 × 20 cm) velveteen, Fabric A
- 4 × 4 inches (10 × 10 cm) cotton, Fabric B
- 2 inches (5 cm) pipe cleaner, dark color
- 7½ inch (15 cm) black yarn
- Embroidery floss, blue
- Stuffing
- Craft glue

MATERIALS FOR 53 SHE-GOAT

- 12 × 8 inches (30 × 20 cm) velveteen, Fabric A
- 4 × 4 inches (10 × 10 cm) cotton, Fabric B
- Embroidery floss, red
- Stuffing
- Craft glue

STEP 1. MAKE THE HEAD

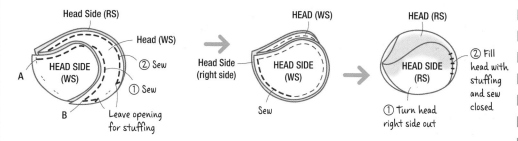

STEP 2. MAKE THE ARMS AND LEGS

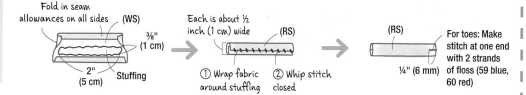

STEP 3. MAKE THE BODY

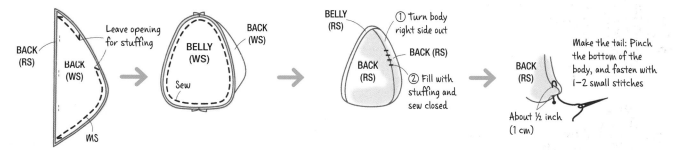

STEP 4. JOIN THE BODY PARTS

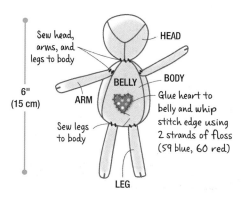

STEP 5. MAKE THE FACE

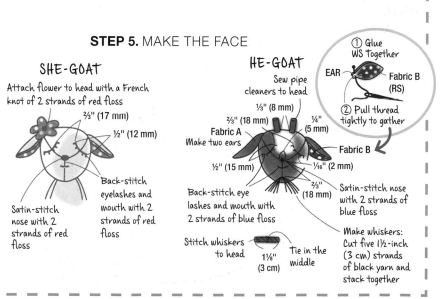

Full pattern on page 143

MATERIALS FOR 54 PRAIRIE BUNNY

- 10 × 6 inches (25 × 15 cm) wool tweed, Fabric A
- 4 × 4 inches (10 × 10 cm) checked wool, Fabric B
- 4 × 4 inches (10 × 10 cm) checked cotton, Fabric C
- 8 × 4 inches (20 × 10 cm) checked gauze, Fabric D
- 2 × 2 inches (5 × 5 cm) flower-print cotton, Fabric E
- 4 × 2 inches (10 × 5 cm) linen, Fabric F
- ¾ × ¾ inches (2 × 2 cm) wool, Fabric G
- ⅝ × ⅝ inches (1 × 1 cm) tweed for eyes, Fabric H
- 2 × 2 inches (5 × 5 cm) pink felt
- One 4-mm button for clothing
- Two 7-mm button for attaching arms
- 5 inches (12 cm) of ¾ inches (2 cm)-wide gathered lace
- 4 inches (10 cm) of ¼ inches (5 mm) lace ribbon
- 13 inches (34 cm) of 1/16 inches (2 mm) ribbon
- 5 inches (12 cm) of ¼ inches (5-mm) nonadhesive hem tape
- Embroidery floss, black and red
- Stuffing

MATERIALS FOR 55 GOOD NIGHT BEAR

- 10 × 6 inches (25 × 15 cm) wool tweed, Fabric A
- 4 × 2 inches (10 × 5 cm) wool print, Fabric B
- 2 × 2 inches (5 × 5 cm) light brown gauze, Fabric C
- 8 × 8 inches (20 × 20 cm) light yellow gauze, Fabric D
- 4 × 4" (10 × 10 cm) cotton, Fabric E
- 2 × 2" (5 × 5 cm) dark brown felt
- Two 4-mm buttons for nightshirt
- Two 7-mm buttons for attaching arms
- 4" (10 cm) pipe cleaner for nightcap
- 4" (10 cm) of ½" (1.5 cm)-wide lace
- Six-strand embroidery floss, white, black, and red
- Stuffing

STEP 1. SEW HEAD

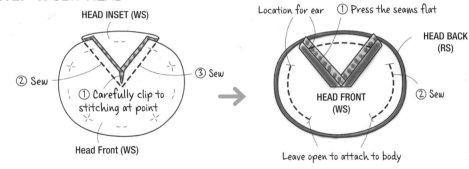

HEAD INSET (WS)

② Sew   ③ Sew
① Carefully clip to stitching at point
Head Front (WS)

Location for ear
① Press the seams flat
HEAD BACK (RS)
② Sew
HEAD FRONT (WS)
② Sew
Leave open to attach to body

STEP 2. MAKE EARS AND ATTACH TO HEAD

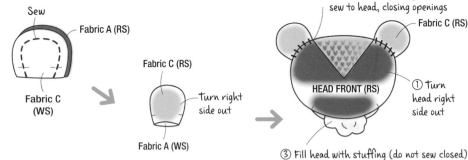

Sew
Fabric A (RS)
Fabric C (WS)
Fabric A (WS)

Fabric C (RS)
Turn right side out

② Place ears at openings and sew to head, closing openings
Fabric C (RS)
① Turn head right side out
HEAD FRONT (RS)
③ Fill head with stuffing (do not sew closed)

STEP 3. MAKE THE LEGS

③ Fill legs with stuffing
① Sew seam and turn right side out
LEG (RS)
② Whip-stitch edges together
BOTTOM OF FOOT (RS)

STEP 4. ATTACH LEGS AND FILL WITH STUFFING

④ Fill body with stuffing
① Sew seam and turn right side out
BODY (RS)
② Fold under seam allowance
③ Insert legs and sew together

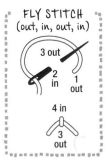

FLY STITCH (out, in, out, in)

3 out
2 in   1 out
4 in
3 out

STEP 5. HOW TO MAKE THE FACE

GOOD NIGHT BEAR

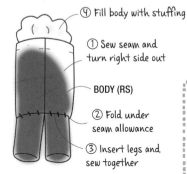

Nose: Satin-stitch with 1 strand of black floss

Eyes: Fly-stitch with 1 strand of white floss

Mouth: Fly-stitch with 1 strand of black floss

Fold under seam allowance and whip stitch to head

PRAIRIE BUNNY

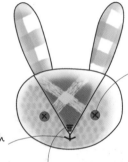

Eyes: Cut 2 circles (¼ inch [0.4 cm]) of Fabric H and attach to head with 2 stitches making an "X"

Nose: Satin-stitch with 1 strand of black floss

SATIN STITCH (out, in, out)

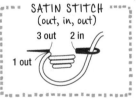

3 out   2 in
1 out

NOSE (RS)
② Fill with stuffing and pull thread tightly to gather
① Baste on seam line
About ½ inch (1.2 cm)

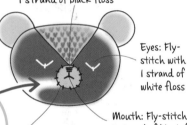

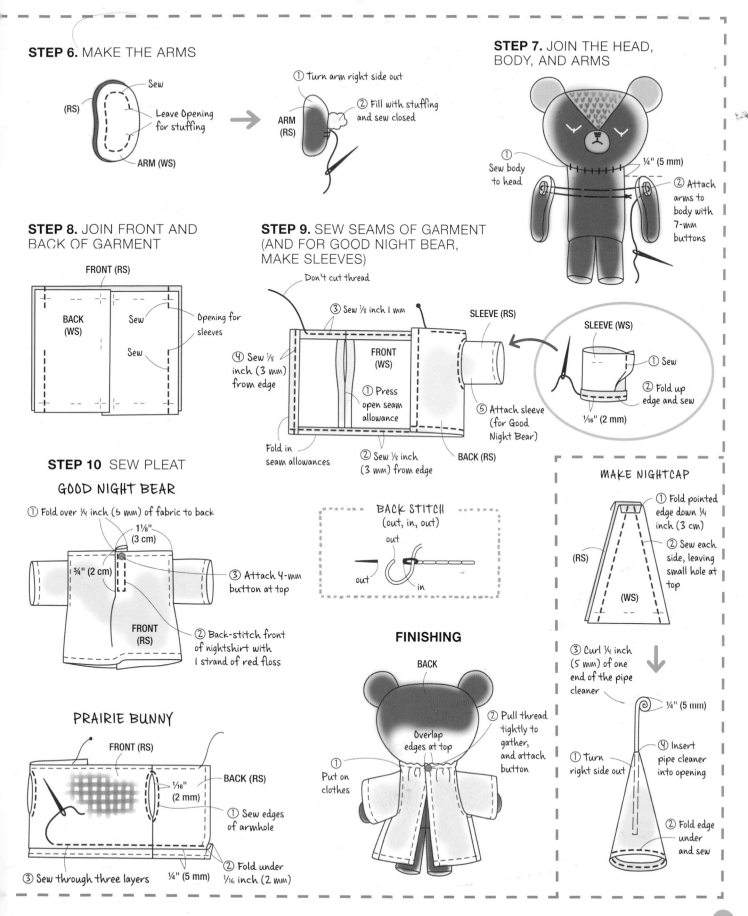

STEP 6. MAKE THE ARMS

Sew
(RS)
Leave Opening for stuffing
ARM (WS)

① Turn arm right side out
② Fill with stuffing and sew closed
ARM (RS)

STEP 7. JOIN THE HEAD, BODY, AND ARMS

① Sew body to head
¼" (5 mm)
② Attach arms to body with 7-mm buttons

STEP 8. JOIN FRONT AND BACK OF GARMENT

FRONT (RS)
BACK (WS)
Sew
Sew
Opening for sleeves

STEP 9. SEW SEAMS OF GARMENT (AND FOR GOOD NIGHT BEAR, MAKE SLEEVES)

Don't cut thread
③ Sew ⅛ inch 1 mm
④ Sew ⅛ inch (3 mm) from edge
FRONT (WS)
① Press open seam allowance
Fold in seam allowances
② Sew ⅛ inch (3 mm) from edge
SLEEVE (RS)
⑤ Attach sleeve (for Good Night Bear)
BACK (RS)

SLEEVE (WS)
① Sew
② Fold up edge and sew
1/16" (2 mm)

STEP 10 SEW PLEAT

GOOD NIGHT BEAR

① Fold over ¼ inch (5 mm) of fabric to back
1⅛" (3 cm)
¾" (2 cm)
③ Attach 4-mm button at top
FRONT (RS)
② Back-stitch front of nightshirt with 1 strand of red floss

BACK STITCH (out, in, out)
out
out
in

PRAIRIE BUNNY

FRONT (RS)
BACK (RS)
1/16" (2 mm)
① Sew edges of armhole
② Fold under 1/16 inch (2 mm)
③ Sew through three layers
¼" (5 mm)

FINISHING

BACK
Overlap edges at top
① Put on clothes
② Pull thread tightly to gather, and attach button

MAKE NIGHTCAP

① Fold pointed edge down ¼ inch (3 cm)
② Sew each side, leaving small hole at top
(RS)
(WS)

③ Curl ¼ inch (5 mm) of one end of the pipe cleaner
¼" (5 mm)
① Turn right side out
④ Insert pipe cleaner into opening
② Fold edge under and sew

STEP 12. MAKE BUNNY'S BONNET

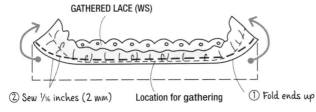

GATHERED LACE (WS)

② Sew 1/16 inches (2 mm)   Location for gathering   ① Fold ends up

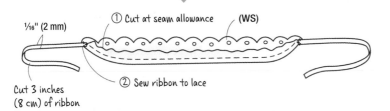

1/16" (2 mm)

① Cut at seam allowance   (WS)

② Sew ribbon to lace

Cut 3 inches
(8 cm) of ribbon

STEP 13. MAKE BUNNY'S APRON

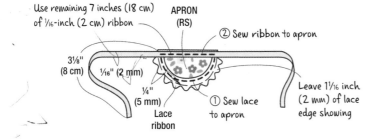

Use remaining 7 inches (18 cm)
of 1/16-inch (2 cm) ribbon

APRON
(RS)

② Sew ribbon to apron

3 1/8"
(8 cm)   1/16" (2 mm)

1/4"
(5 mm)

Lace
ribbon

① Sew lace
to apron

Leave 1 1/16 inch
(2 mm) of lace
edge showing

STEP 14. MAKE BEAR'S PILLOW

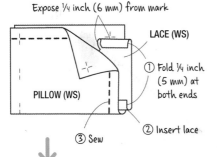

Expose 1/4 inch (6 mm) from mark

LACE (WS)

① Fold 1/4 inch
(5 mm) at
both ends

PILLOW (WS)

② Insert lace

③ Sew

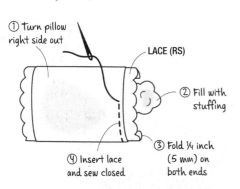

① Turn pillow
right side out

LACE (RS)

② Fill with
stuffing

④ Insert lace
and sew closed

③ Fold 1/4 inch
(5 mm) on
both ends

STEP 15. MAKE BUNNY'S BAG

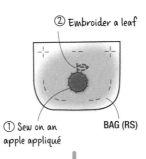

② Embroider a leaf

① Sew on an
apple appliqué

BAG (RS)

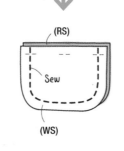

(RS)

Sew

(WS)

④ Sew 2 1/2 inches
(6 cm) of hem
tape to inside of
top of bag

1/4" (5 mm)

② Fold in seam
allowance

1/16"
(2 mm)

① Turn right side out

③ Back-stitch with
1 strand of red floss

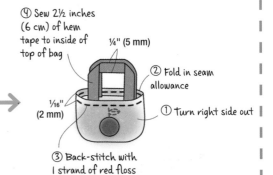

FINISHING
GOOD NIGHT BEAR

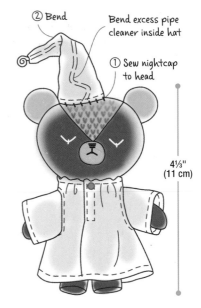

② Bend

Bend excess pipe
cleaner inside hat

① Sew nightcap
to head

4 1/3"
(11 cm)

PRAIRIE BUNNY

Sew bonnet
loosely to head

5 1/8"
(13 cm)

Tie apron in back

Patterns for 1 Marin and 2 Sky, page 6

Bold line is seam line, outside line is cutting line

NOTE: Mirror images of some pattern pieces are needed for the right and left sides of the creature, so cut one pattern on the fabric's right side and one pattern on the fabric's wrong side.

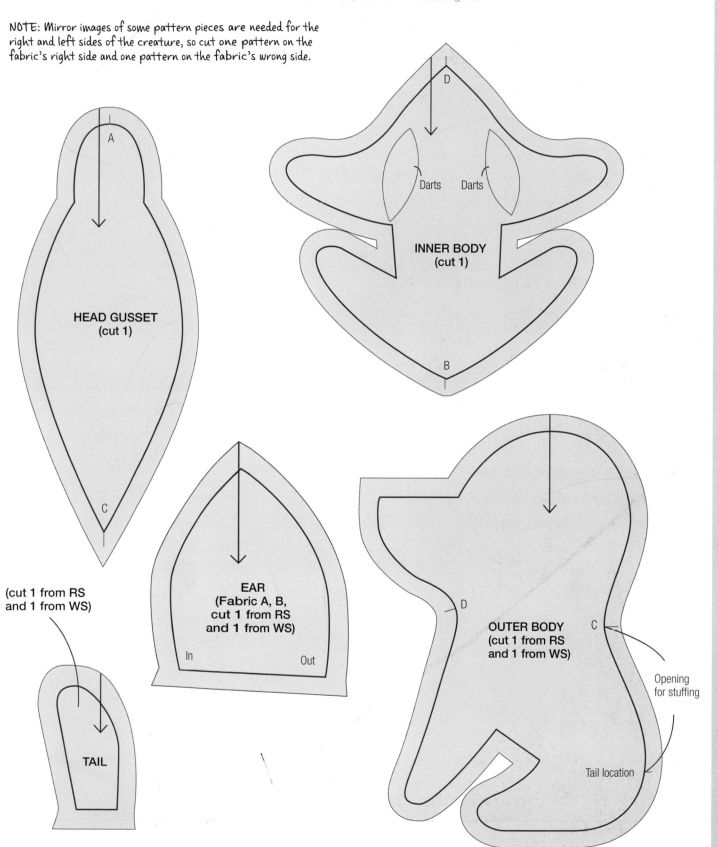

A

HEAD GUSSET
(cut 1)

C

D

Darts   Darts

INNER BODY
(cut 1)

B

EAR
(Fabric A, B,
cut 1 from RS
and 1 from WS)

In   Out

(cut 1 from RS
and 1 from WS)

TAIL

D

OUTER BODY
(cut 1 from RS
and 1 from WS)

C

Opening
for stuffing

Tail location

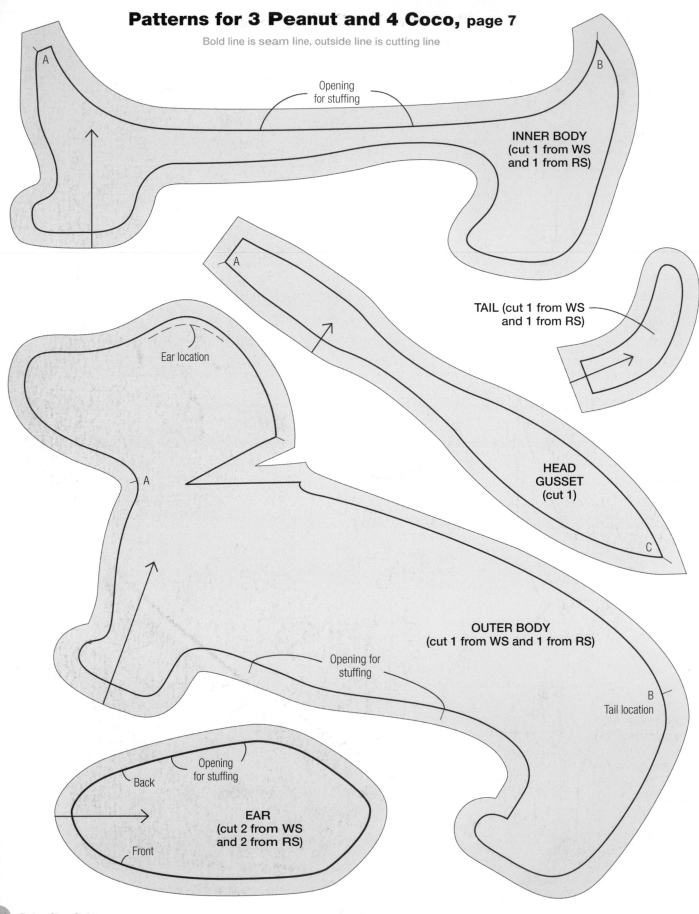

Patterns for 3 Peanut and 4 Coco, page 7

Bold line is seam line, outside line is cutting line

A

B

Opening
for stuffing

INNER BODY
(cut 1 from WS
and 1 from RS)

A

TAIL (cut 1 from WS
and 1 from RS)

Ear location

A

HEAD
GUSSET
(cut 1)

C

A

OUTER BODY
(cut 1 from WS and 1 from RS)

Opening for
stuffing

B
Tail location

Opening
for stuffing

Back

EAR
(cut 2 from WS
and 2 from RS)

Front

Patterns for 5 Max, page 7

Bold line is seam line, outside line is cutting line

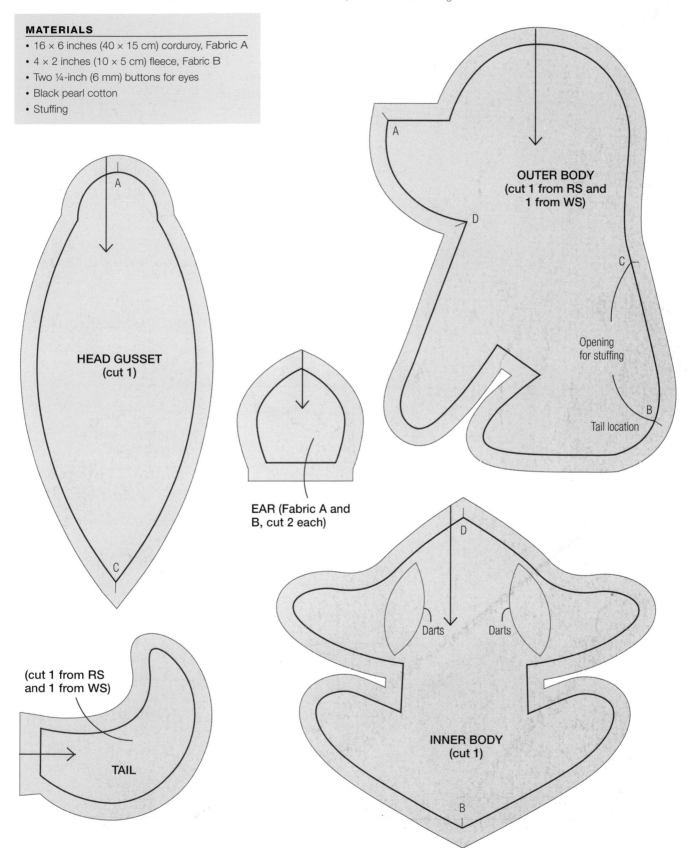

MATERIALS
- 16 × 6 inches (40 × 15 cm) corduroy, Fabric A
- 4 × 2 inches (10 × 5 cm) fleece, Fabric B
- Two ¼-inch (6 mm) buttons for eyes
- Black pearl cotton
- Stuffing

A

HEAD GUSSET
(cut 1)

C

OUTER BODY
(cut 1 from RS and
1 from WS)

A

D

C

Opening
for stuffing

B

Tail location

EAR (Fabric A and
B, cut 2 each)

(cut 1 from RS
and 1 from WS)

TAIL

INNER BODY
(cut 1)

D

Darts   Darts

B

Patterns for 6 Billy, page 8

Bold line is seam line, line outside is cutting line

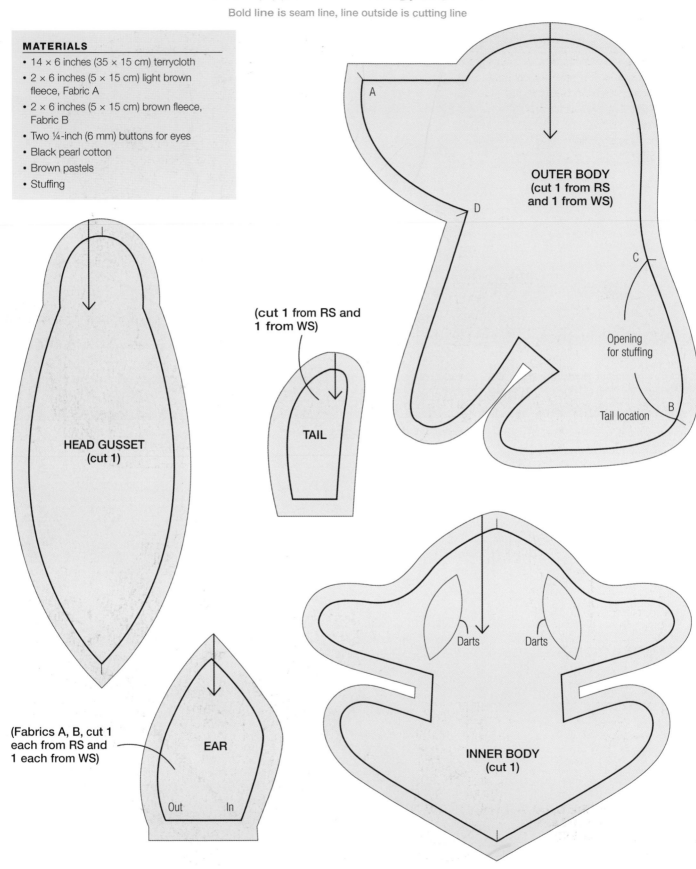

MATERIALS

- 14 × 6 inches (35 × 15 cm) terrycloth
- 2 × 6 inches (5 × 15 cm) light brown fleece, Fabric A
- 2 × 6 inches (5 × 15 cm) brown fleece, Fabric B
- Two ¼-inch (6 mm) buttons for eyes
- Black pearl cotton
- Brown pastels
- Stuffing

A

D

OUTER BODY
(cut 1 from RS and 1 from WS)

C

Opening for stuffing

B

Tail location

HEAD GUSSET
(cut 1)

(cut 1 from RS and 1 from WS)

TAIL

(Fabrics A, B, cut 1 each from RS and 1 each from WS)

EAR

Out   In

Darts   Darts

INNER BODY
(cut 1)

Patterns for 7 Jimmy, page 8

Bold line is seam line, outside line is cutting line

MATERIALS
- 8 × 10 inches (20 × 25 cm) white felt, Fabric A
- 4 × 2 inches (10 × 5 cm) pink felt, Fabric B
- 4 × 2 inches (10 × 5 cm) black felt, Fabric C
- Two ¼-inch (5 mm) buttons for eyes
- Black pearl cotton
- Black and orange pastels
- Stuffing

EAR

In   Out

(Fabric B, cut 1 from
RS and 1 from WS)
(Fabric C, Left Outer
Ear, cut 1)
(Fabric A, Right Outer
Ear, cut 1)

A

HEAD GUSSET
(cut 1)

C

A

OUTER BODY
(cut 1 from RS and
1 from WS)

D

C

Opening
for stuffing

Tail
location

B

D

Darts   Darts

INNER
BODY
(cut 1)

B

TAIL

(Fabric C, cut 1
from RS and 1
from WS)

Patterns for 8 Olga and 9 Pedro, page 9

Bold line is seam line, outside line is cutting line

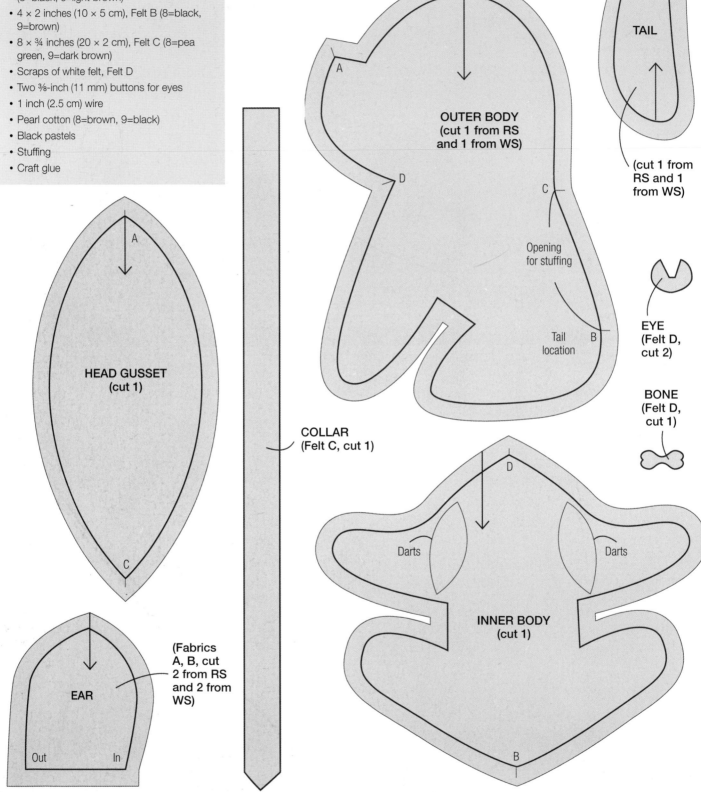

MATERIALS

- 10 × 10 inches (25 × 25 cm), Felt A (8=black, 9=light brown)
- 4 × 2 inches (10 × 5 cm), Felt B (8=black, 9=brown)
- 8 × ¾ inches (20 × 2 cm), Felt C (8=pea green, 9=dark brown)
- Scraps of white felt, Felt D
- Two ⅜-inch (11 mm) buttons for eyes
- 1 inch (2.5 cm) wire
- Pearl cotton (8=brown, 9=black)
- Black pastels
- Stuffing
- Craft glue

HEAD GUSSET
(cut 1)

A

C

EAR

Out   In

(Fabrics A, B, cut 2 from RS and 2 from WS)

COLLAR
(Felt C, cut 1)

OUTER BODY
(cut 1 from RS and 1 from WS)

A

D

C

Opening for stuffing

Tail location

B

TAIL

(cut 1 from RS and 1 from WS)

EYE
(Felt D, cut 2)

BONE
(Felt D, cut 1)

INNER BODY
(cut 1)

D

Darts

Darts

B

Patterns for 10 Dudley and 11 Arthur, pages 10–11

Bold line is seam line, outside line is cutting line

NOTE: Pattern pieces for body, arms, legs, and ears are different for 10 Dudley and 11 Arthur. Dudley's parts are made separately, and Arthur has only separate ears.

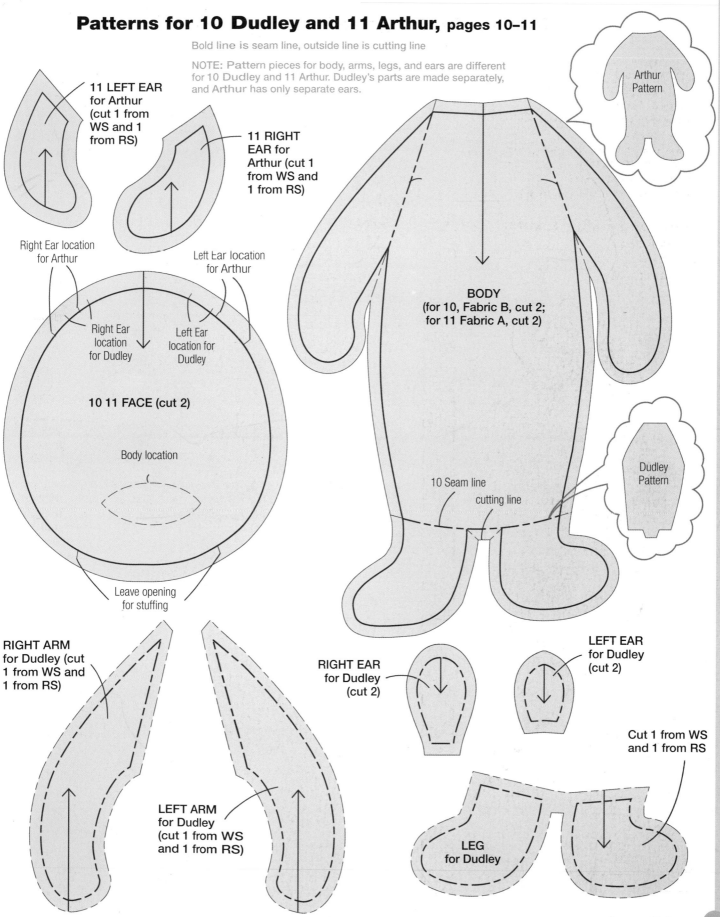

11 LEFT EAR for Arthur (cut 1 from WS and 1 from RS)

11 RIGHT EAR for Arthur (cut 1 from WS and 1 from RS)

Arthur Pattern

Right Ear location for Arthur

Left Ear location for Arthur

Right Ear location for Dudley

Left Ear location for Dudley

10 11 FACE (cut 2)

Body location

Leave opening for stuffing

BODY
(for 10, Fabric B, cut 2; for 11 Fabric A, cut 2)

10 Seam line

cutting line

Dudley Pattern

RIGHT ARM for Dudley (cut 1 from WS and 1 from RS)

LEFT ARM for Dudley (cut 1 from WS and 1 from RS)

RIGHT EAR for Dudley (cut 2)

LEFT EAR for Dudley (cut 2)

Cut 1 from WS and 1 from RS

LEG for Dudley

Patterns for 12 Charlie and 13 Randy, page 12

Bold line is seam line, outside line is cutting line

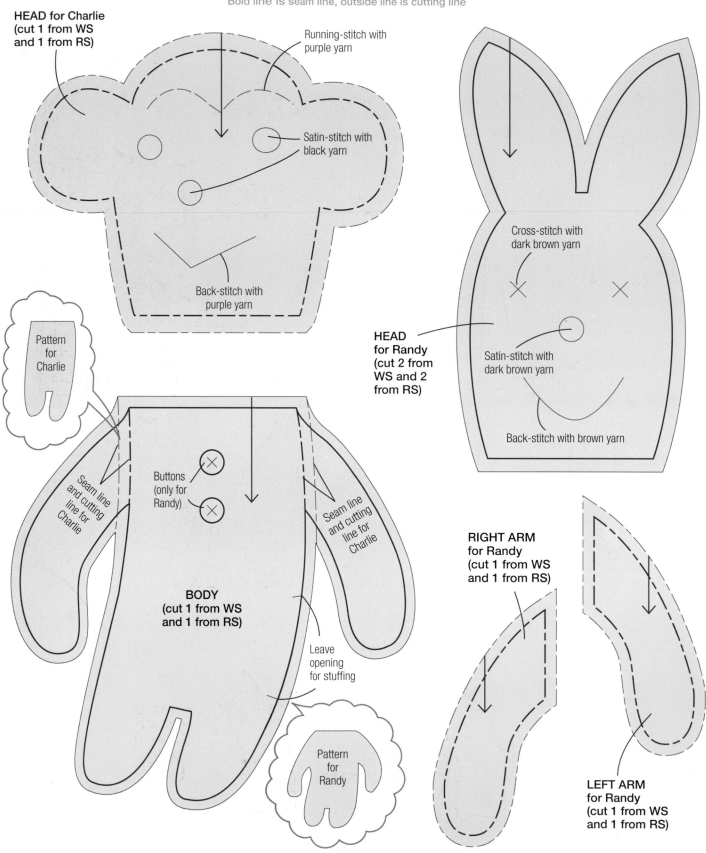

HEAD for Charlie
(cut 1 from WS
and 1 from RS)

Running-stitch with
purple yarn

Satin-stitch with
black yarn

Back-stitch with
purple yarn

Pattern
for
Charlie

Cross-stitch with
dark brown yarn

HEAD
for Randy
(cut 2 from
WS and 2
from RS)

Satin-stitch with
dark brown yarn

Back-stitch with brown yarn

Seam line
and cutting
line for
Charlie

Buttons
(only for
Randy)

Seam line
and cutting
line for
Charlie

BODY
(cut 1 from WS
and 1 from RS)

Leave
opening
for stuffing

Pattern
for
Randy

RIGHT ARM
for Randy
(cut 1 from WS
and 1 from RS)

LEFT ARM
for Randy
(cut 1 from WS
and 1 from RS)

Bold line is seam line, outside line is cutting line

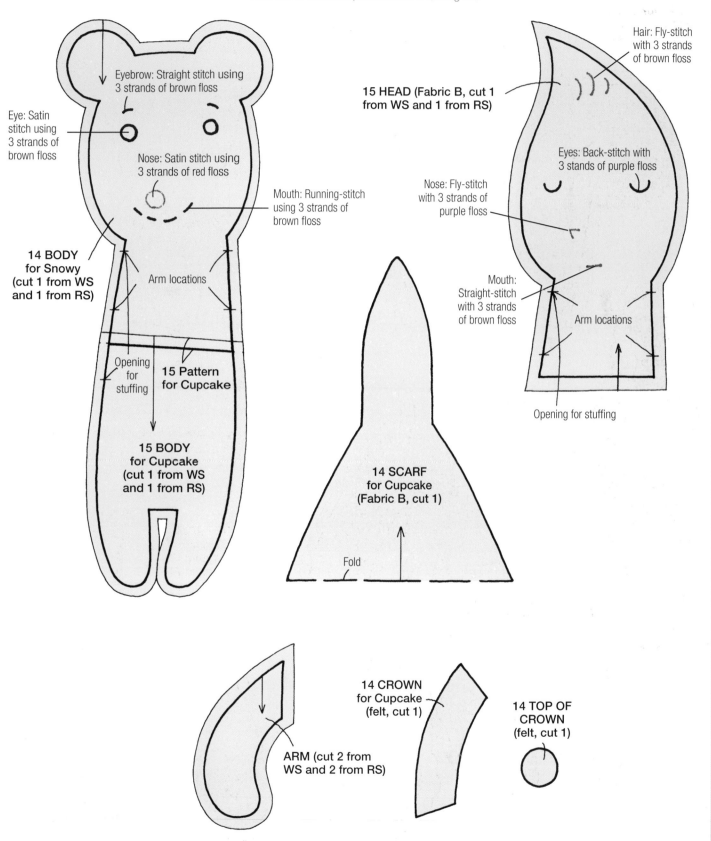

Eyebrow: Straight stitch using 3 strands of brown floss

Eye: Satin stitch using 3 strands of brown floss

Nose: Satin stitch using 3 strands of red floss

Mouth: Running-stitch using 3 strands of brown floss

14 BODY for Snowy (cut 1 from WS and 1 from RS)

Arm locations

Opening for stuffing

15 Pattern for Cupcake

15 BODY for Cupcake (cut 1 from WS and 1 from RS)

15 HEAD (Fabric B, cut 1 from WS and 1 from RS)

Hair: Fly-stitch with 3 strands of brown floss

Eyes: Back-stitch with 3 stands of purple floss

Nose: Fly-stitch with 3 strands of purple floss

Mouth: Straight-stitch with 3 strands of brown floss

Arm locations

Opening for stuffing

14 SCARF for Cupcake (Fabric B, cut 1)

Fold

ARM (cut 2 from WS and 2 from RS)

14 CROWN for Cupcake (felt, cut 1)

14 TOP OF CROWN (felt, cut 1)

Bold line is seam line, outside line is cutting line

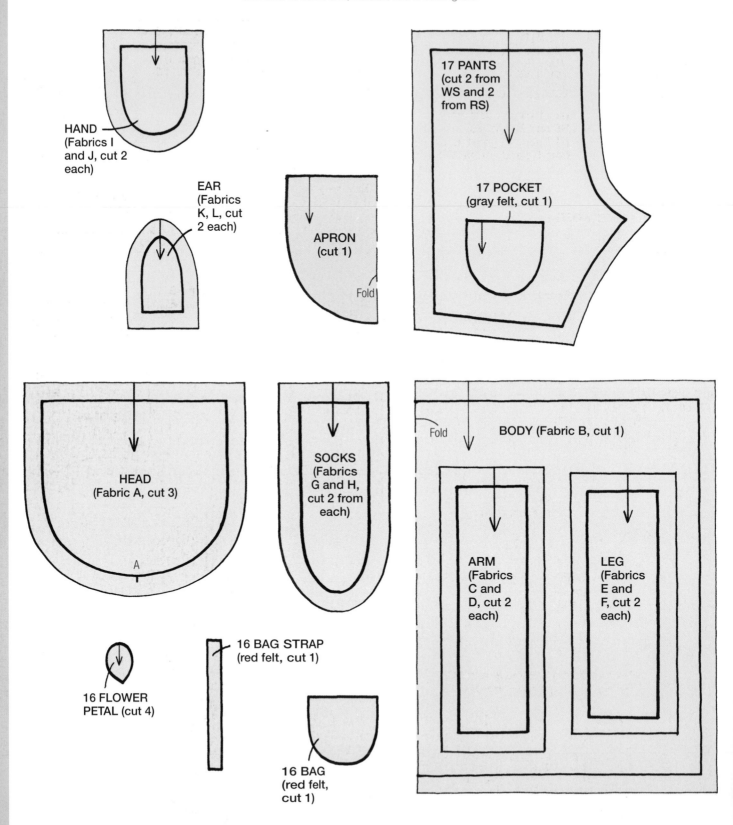

HAND
(Fabrics I
and J, cut 2
each)

EAR
(Fabrics
K, L, cut
2 each)

APRON
(cut 1)

Fold

17 PANTS
(cut 2 from
WS and 2
from RS)

17 POCKET
(gray felt, cut 1)

HEAD
(Fabric A, cut 3)

A

SOCKS
(Fabrics
G and H,
cut 2 from
each)

Fold

BODY (Fabric B, cut 1)

ARM
(Fabrics
C and
D, cut 2
each)

LEG
(Fabrics
E and
F, cut 2
each)

16 FLOWER
PETAL (cut 4)

16 BAG STRAP
(red felt, cut 1)

16 BAG
(red felt,
cut 1)

Patterns for 18 Huang Huang, 19 Henry, 20 Minou, pages 16–17

Bold line is seam line, outside line is cutting line

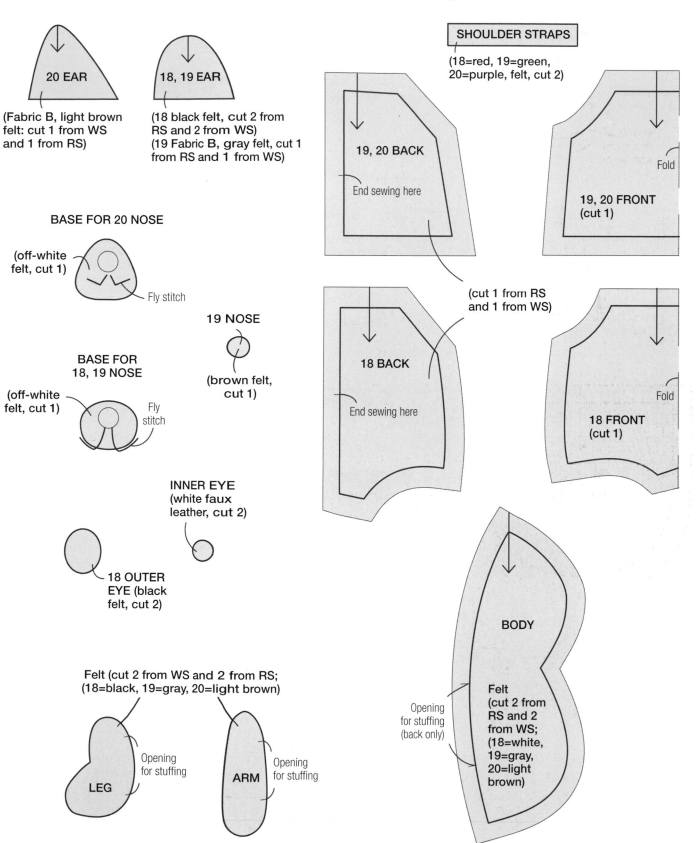

20 EAR

(Fabric B, light brown felt: cut 1 from WS and 1 from RS)

18, 19 EAR

(18 black felt, cut 2 from RS and 2 from WS)
(19 Fabric B, gray felt, cut 1 from RS and 1 from WS)

SHOULDER STRAPS

(18=red, 19=green, 20=purple, felt, cut 2)

19, 20 BACK

End sewing here

19, 20 FRONT (cut 1)

Fold

BASE FOR 20 NOSE

(off-white felt, cut 1)

Fly stitch

(cut 1 from RS and 1 from WS)

18 BACK

End sewing here

18 FRONT (cut 1)

Fold

19 NOSE

(brown felt, cut 1)

BASE FOR 18, 19 NOSE

(off-white felt, cut 1)

Fly stitch

INNER EYE (white faux leather, cut 2)

18 OUTER EYE (black felt, cut 2)

Felt (cut 2 from WS and 2 from RS; (18=black, 19=gray, 20=light brown)

Opening for stuffing

LEG

ARM

Opening for stuffing

BODY

Opening for stuffing (back only)

Felt (cut 2 from RS and 2 from WS; (18=white, 19=gray, 20=light brown)

Patterns for 21 Toby, 22 Gigi, and 23 Kate, pages 18–19

Bold line is seam line, outside line is cutting line

21, 22, 23 Patterns

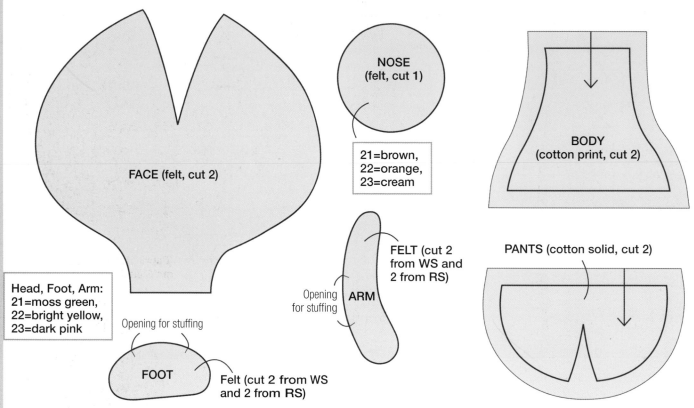

FACE (felt, cut 2)

NOSE
(felt, cut 1)

21=brown,
22=orange,
23=cream

Head, Foot, Arm:
21=moss green,
22=bright yellow,
23=dark pink

FELT (cut 2
from WS and
2 from RS)

Opening
for stuffing

ARM

BODY
(cotton print, cut 2)

PANTS (cotton solid, cut 2)

Opening for stuffing

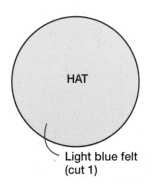

FOOT

Felt (cut 2 from WS
and 2 from RS)

21 Toby Patterns

Hat Side

Black felt (cut 1)

Hat Brim

Black felt
(cut 1)

Hat Top

Black felt
(cut 1)

Brown felt
(cut 2 from
WS and 2
from RS)

EAR

22 Gigi Patterns

HAT

Light blue felt
(cut 1)

EAR

Bright yellow felt
(cut 2 from WS
and 2 from RS)

23 Kate Patterns

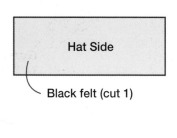

EAR

Dark pink felt
(cut 2 from
WS and 2
from RS)

FLOWER

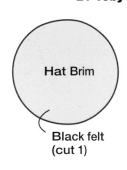

Purple felt (cut 1)

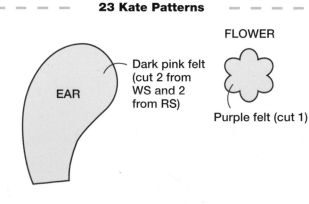

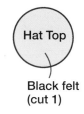

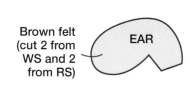

Patterns for 24 Fawn and 25 Pony, page 20

Bold line is seam line, outside line is cutting line

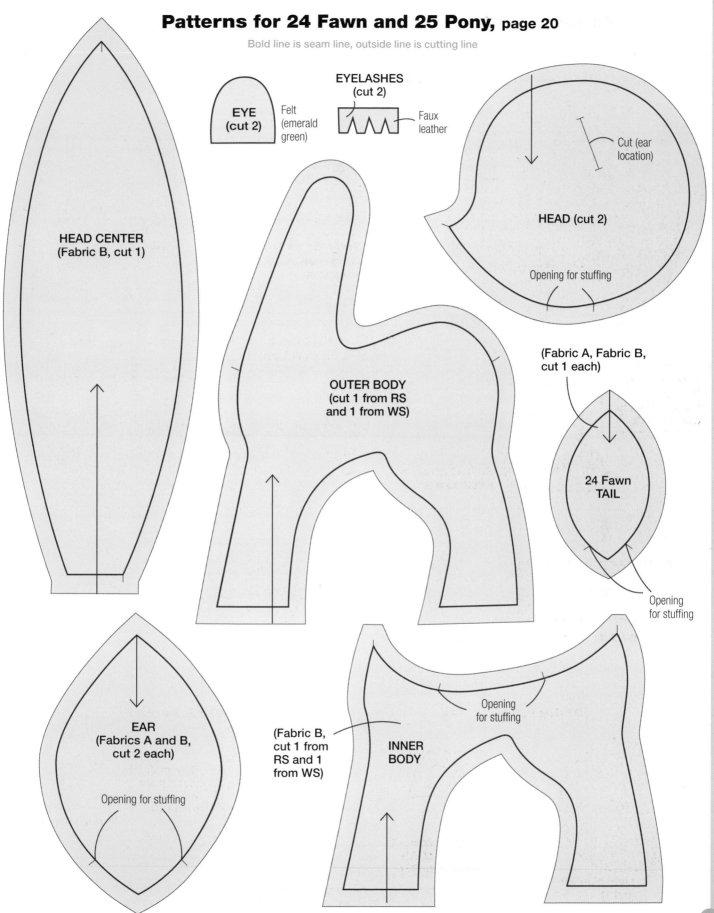

HEAD CENTER
(Fabric B, cut 1)

EYE (cut 2)

Felt (emerald green)

EYELASHES (cut 2)

Faux leather

HEAD (cut 2)

Cut (ear location)

Opening for stuffing

OUTER BODY
(cut 1 from RS and 1 from WS)

(Fabric A, Fabric B, cut 1 each)

24 Fawn TAIL

Opening for stuffing

EAR
(Fabrics A and B, cut 2 each)

Opening for stuffing

(Fabric B, cut 1 from RS and 1 from WS)

INNER BODY

Opening for stuffing

Patterns for 26 Bunny and 27 Squirrel, page 21

Bold line is seam line, outside line is cutting line

26, 27 Patterns (26=Fabric B, 27=Fabric A)

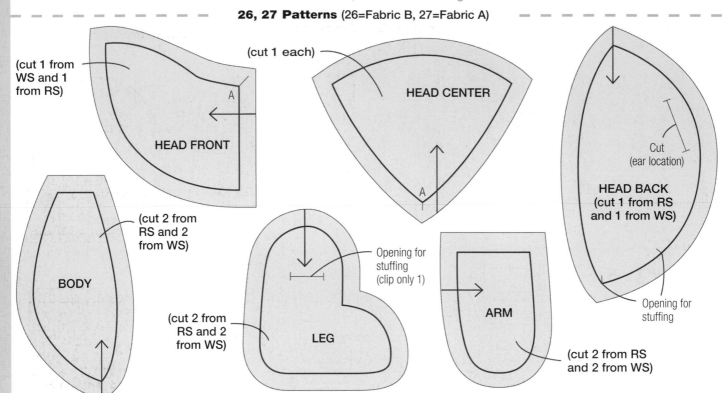

(cut 1 from WS and 1 from RS)

HEAD FRONT

A

(cut 1 each)

HEAD CENTER

A

Cut (ear location)

HEAD BACK (cut 1 from RS and 1 from WS)

Opening for stuffing

(cut 2 from RS and 2 from WS)

BODY

Opening for stuffing (clip only 1)

(cut 2 from RS and 2 from WS)

LEG

ARM

(cut 2 from RS and 2 from WS)

---

26 Bunny Patterns

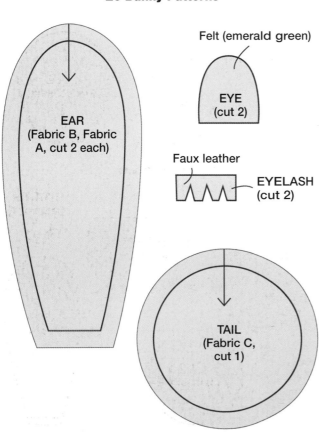

EAR (Fabric B, Fabric A, cut 2 each)

Felt (emerald green)

EYE (cut 2)

Faux leather

EYELASH (cut 2)

TAIL (Fabric C, cut 1)

---

27 Squirrel Patterns

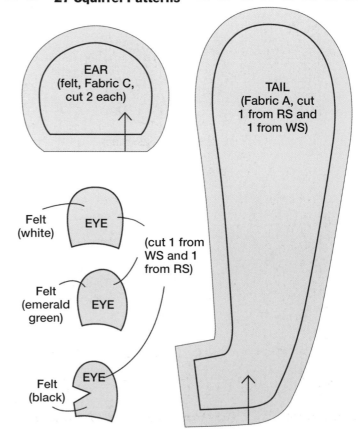

EAR (felt, Fabric C, cut 2 each)

TAIL (Fabric A, cut 1 from RS and 1 from WS)

Felt (white)

EYE

Felt (emerald green)

EYE

(cut 1 from WS and 1 from RS)

Felt (black)

EYE

Patterns for 28 Anders and 29 Zoe, page 22

Bold line is seam line, outside line is cutting line

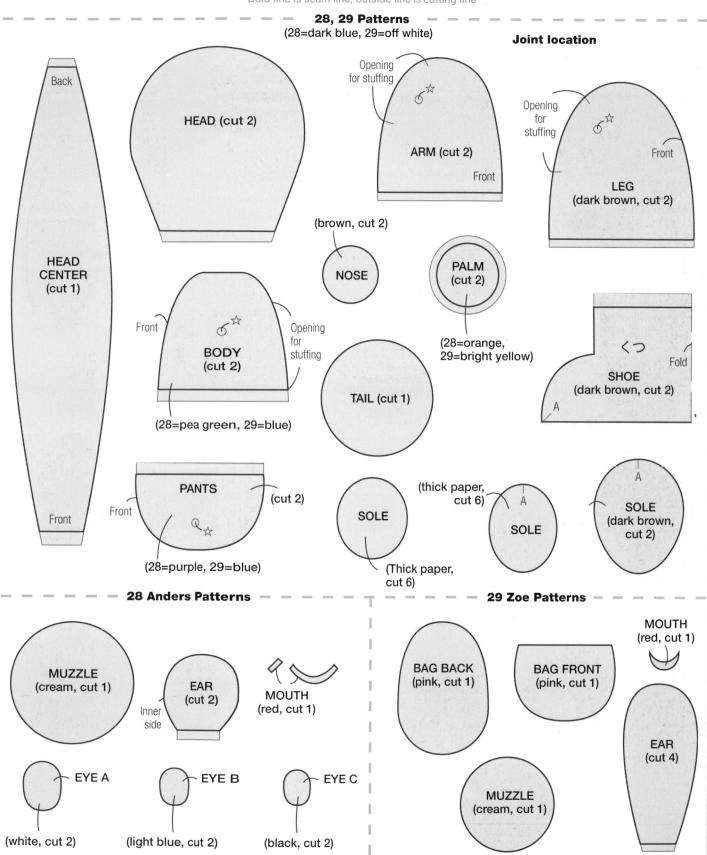

28, 29 Patterns
(28=dark blue, 29=off white)

Joint location

Back

HEAD (cut 2)

Opening for stuffing

ARM (cut 2)

Front

Opening for stuffing

Front

LEG
(dark brown, cut 2)

HEAD CENTER
(cut 1)

(brown, cut 2)

NOSE

PALM
(cut 2)

Front

BODY
(cut 2)

Opening for stuffing

(28=orange,
29=bright yellow)

SHOE
(dark brown, cut 2)

Fold

A

(28=pea green, 29=blue)

TAIL (cut 1)

Front

PANTS

(cut 2)

Front

A

SOLE

(thick paper,
cut 6)

A

SOLE

SOLE
(dark brown,
cut 2)

(28=purple, 29=blue)

(Thick paper,
cut 6)

28 Anders Patterns

MUZZLE
(cream, cut 1)

EAR
(cut 2)

Inner side

MOUTH
(red, cut 1)

EYE A

EYE B

EYE C

(white, cut 2)

(light blue, cut 2)

(black, cut 2)

29 Zoe Patterns

MOUTH
(red, cut 1)

BAG BACK
(pink, cut 1)

BAG FRONT
(pink, cut 1)

EAR
(cut 4)

MUZZLE
(cream, cut 1)

Patterns for 30 Kenken and 31 Mimi, page 23

Bold line is seam line, outside line is cutting line

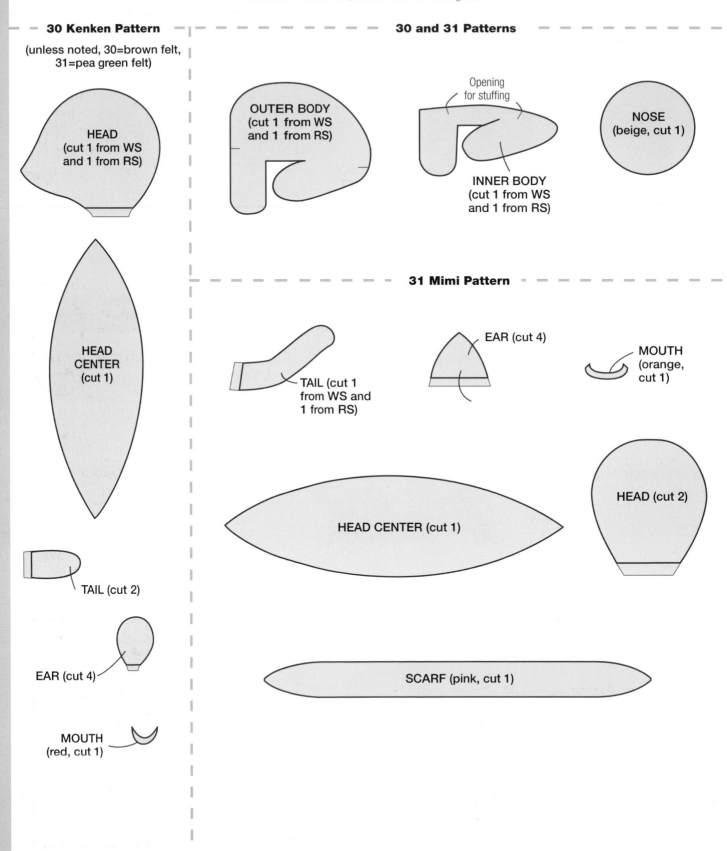

30 Kenken Pattern

(unless noted, 30=brown felt, 31=pea green felt)

HEAD
(cut 1 from WS
and 1 from RS)

HEAD
CENTER
(cut 1)

TAIL (cut 2)

EAR (cut 4)

MOUTH
(red, cut 1)

30 and 31 Patterns

OUTER BODY
(cut 1 from WS
and 1 from RS)

Opening
for stuffing

INNER BODY
(cut 1 from WS
and 1 from RS)

NOSE
(beige, cut 1)

31 Mimi Pattern

TAIL (cut 1
from WS and
1 from RS)

EAR (cut 4)

MOUTH
(orange,
cut 1)

HEAD CENTER (cut 1)

HEAD (cut 2)

SCARF (pink, cut 1)

Patterns for 32 Violet and 33 Palmer, page 24

Bold line is seam line, outside line is cutting line

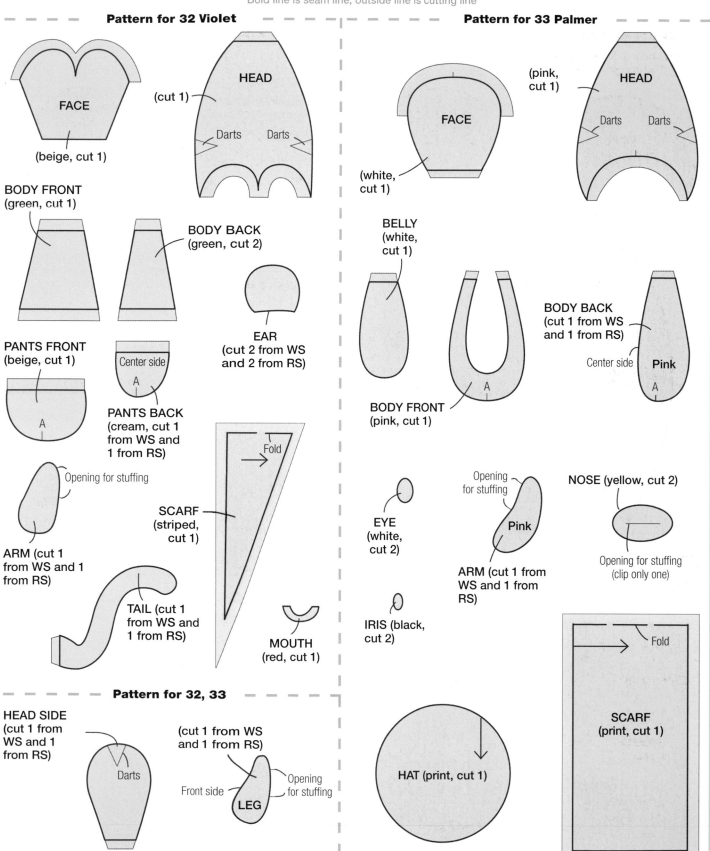

Pattern for 32 Violet

FACE
(beige, cut 1)

HEAD
(cut 1)

Darts   Darts

BODY FRONT
(green, cut 1)

BODY BACK
(green, cut 2)

PANTS FRONT
(beige, cut 1)

Center side
A

PANTS BACK
(cream, cut 1
from WS and
1 from RS)

EAR
(cut 2 from WS
and 2 from RS)

A

Opening for stuffing

SCARF
(striped,
cut 1)

Fold

ARM (cut 1
from WS and 1
from RS)

TAIL (cut 1
from WS and
1 from RS)

MOUTH
(red, cut 1)

Pattern for 33 Palmer

(pink,
cut 1)

FACE

HEAD

Darts   Darts

(white,
cut 1)

BELLY
(white,
cut 1)

BODY BACK
(cut 1 from WS
and 1 from RS)

Center side   Pink

A

BODY FRONT
(pink, cut 1)

A

Opening
for stuffing

EYE
(white,
cut 2)

Pink

ARM (cut 1 from
WS and 1 from
RS)

IRIS (black,
cut 2)

NOSE (yellow, cut 2)

Opening for stuffing
(clip only one)

Fold

SCARF
(print, cut 1)

Pattern for 32, 33

HEAD SIDE
(cut 1 from
WS and 1
from RS)

Darts

(cut 1 from WS
and 1 from RS)

Front side

Opening
for stuffing

LEG

HAT (print, cut 1)

Patterns for 34 Betsy, page 25

Bold line is seam line, outside line is cutting line

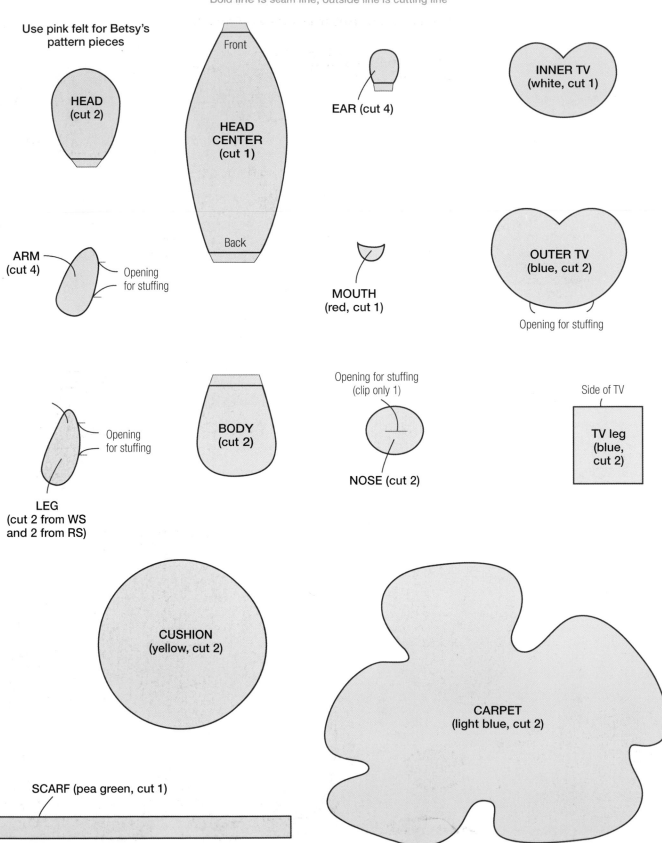

Use pink felt for Betsy's pattern pieces

HEAD (cut 2)

Front

HEAD CENTER (cut 1)

Back

EAR (cut 4)

INNER TV (white, cut 1)

ARM (cut 4)

Opening for stuffing

MOUTH (red, cut 1)

OUTER TV (blue, cut 2)

Opening for stuffing

Opening for stuffing

LEG (cut 2 from WS and 2 from RS)

BODY (cut 2)

Opening for stuffing (clip only 1)

NOSE (cut 2)

Side of TV

TV leg (blue, cut 2)

CUSHION (yellow, cut 2)

CARPET (light blue, cut 2)

SCARF (pea green, cut 1)

Patterns for 35 Piglet, page 27

Bold line is seam line, outside line is cutting line

Unless noted, cut pattern pieces from Fabric A.

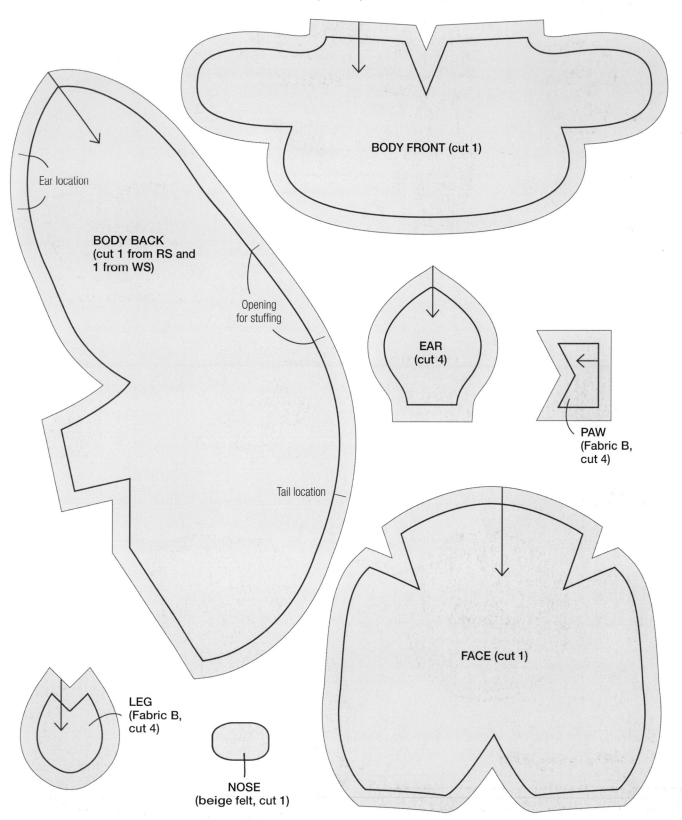

BODY FRONT (cut 1)

Ear location

BODY BACK
(cut 1 from RS and
1 from WS)

Opening
for stuffing

Tail location

EAR
(cut 4)

PAW
(Fabric B,
cut 4)

LEG
(Fabric B,
cut 4)

NOSE
(beige felt, cut 1)

FACE (cut 1)

Bold line is seam line, outside line is cutting line

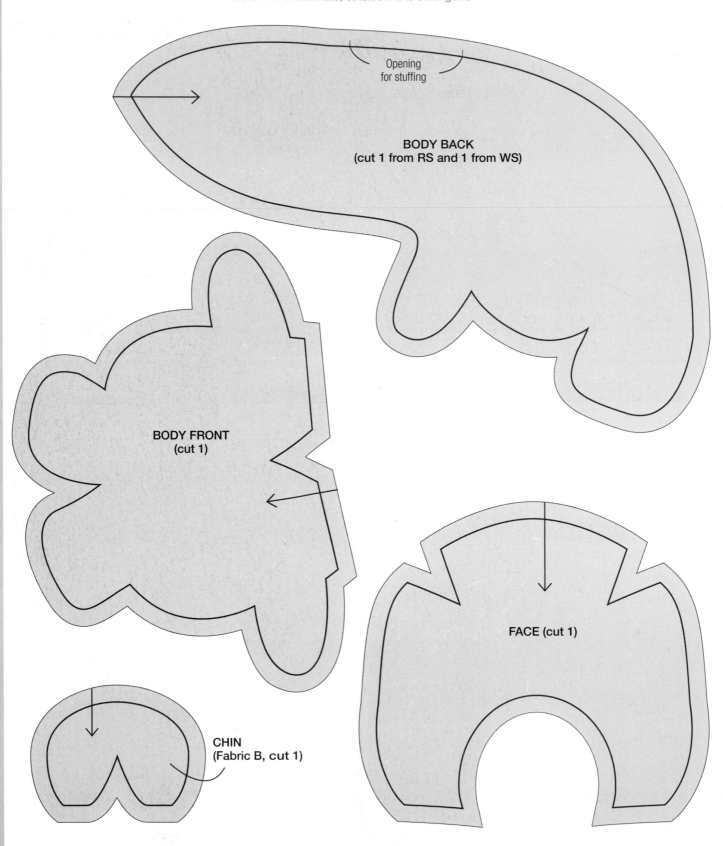

Opening
for stuffing

BODY BACK
(cut 1 from RS and 1 from WS)

BODY FRONT
(cut 1)

FACE (cut 1)

CHIN
(Fabric B, cut 1)

Patterns for 37 Hamster, page 27

Bold line is seam line, outside line is cutting line

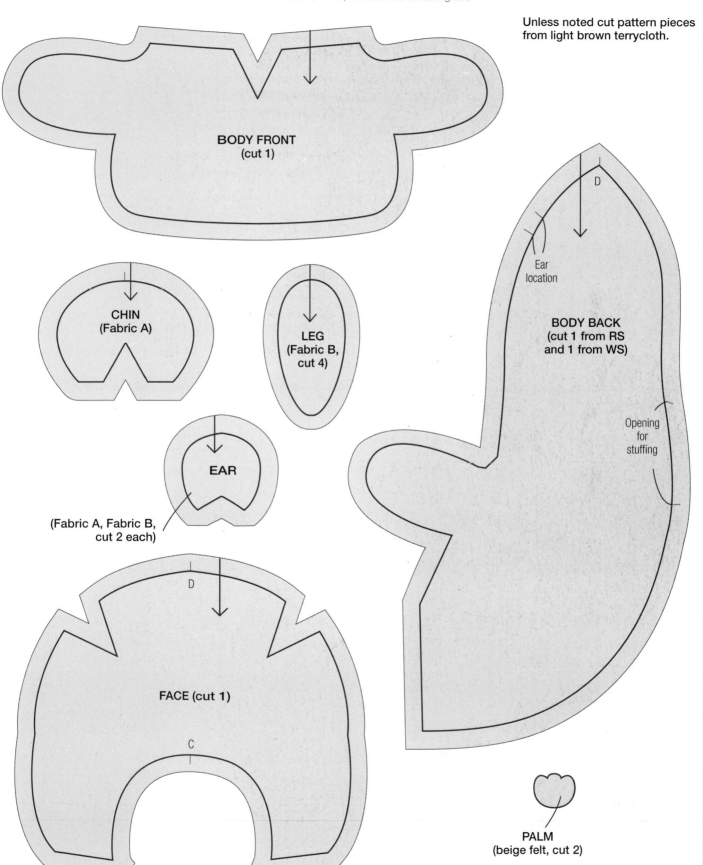

Unless noted cut pattern pieces from light brown terrycloth.

BODY FRONT
(cut 1)

CHIN
(Fabric A)

LEG
(Fabric B,
cut 4)

D

Ear
location

BODY BACK
(cut 1 from RS
and 1 from WS)

Opening
for
stuffing

EAR

(Fabric A, Fabric B,
cut 2 each)

D

FACE (cut 1)

C

PALM
(beige felt, cut 2)

Patterns for 38 Panda, page 27

Bold line is seam line, outside line is cutting line

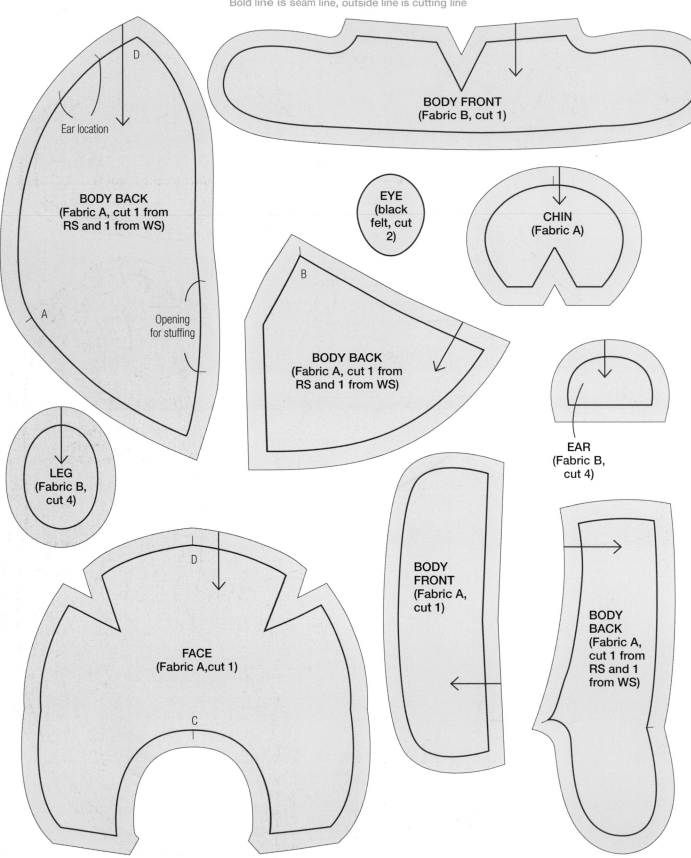

D

Ear location

BODY BACK
(Fabric A, cut 1 from
RS and 1 from WS)

A

Opening
for stuffing

BODY FRONT
(Fabric B, cut 1)

EYE
(black
felt, cut
2)

CHIN
(Fabric A)

B

BODY BACK
(Fabric A, cut 1 from
RS and 1 from WS)

EAR
(Fabric B,
cut 4)

LEG
(Fabric B,
cut 4)

D

FACE
(Fabric A, cut 1)

C

BODY
FRONT
(Fabric A,
cut 1)

BODY
BACK
(Fabric A,
cut 1 from
RS and 1
from WS)

Patterns for 39 Frog, page 27

Bold line is seam line, outside line is cutting line

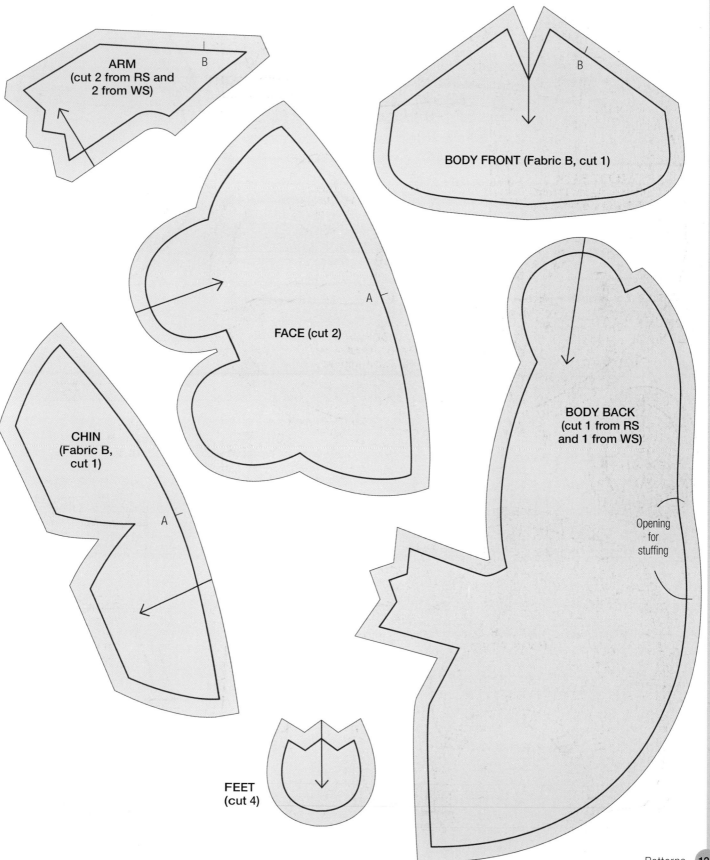

ARM
(cut 2 from RS and
2 from WS)

B

BODY FRONT (Fabric B, cut 1)

B

FACE (cut 2)

A

BODY BACK
(cut 1 from RS
and 1 from WS)

CHIN
(Fabric B,
cut 1)

A

Opening
for
stuffing

FEET
(cut 4)

Patterns for 40 Kiki, 41 Hana, 42 Nick, page 29

Bold line is seam line, outside line is cutting line

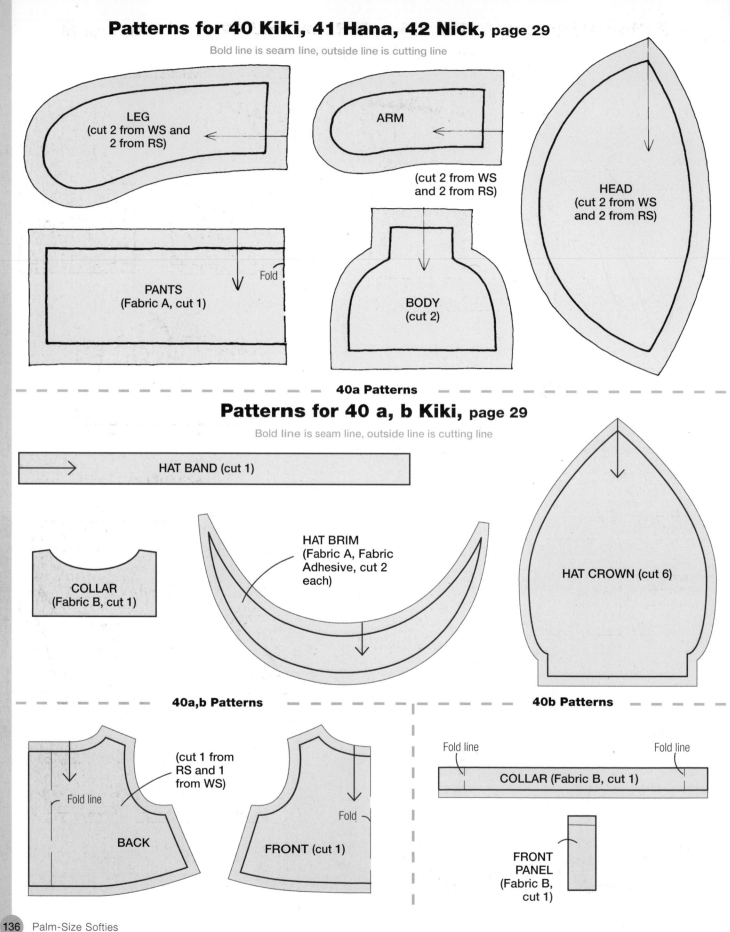

LEG
(cut 2 from WS and
2 from RS)

ARM
(cut 2 from WS
and 2 from RS)

HEAD
(cut 2 from WS
and 2 from RS)

PANTS
(Fabric A, cut 1)

Fold

BODY
(cut 2)

40a Patterns

Patterns for 40 a, b Kiki, page 29

Bold line is seam line, outside line is cutting line

HAT BAND (cut 1)

COLLAR
(Fabric B, cut 1)

HAT BRIM
(Fabric A, Fabric
Adhesive, cut 2
each)

HAT CROWN (cut 6)

40a,b Patterns   **40b Patterns**

(cut 1 from
RS and 1
from WS)

Fold line

BACK

Fold

FRONT (cut 1)

Fold line   Fold line

COLLAR (Fabric B, cut 1)

FRONT
PANEL
(Fabric B,
cut 1)

Patterns for 40 a, b Kiki, 41 a, b Hana, and 42 a, b Nick, page 29

Bold line is seam line, outside line is cutting line

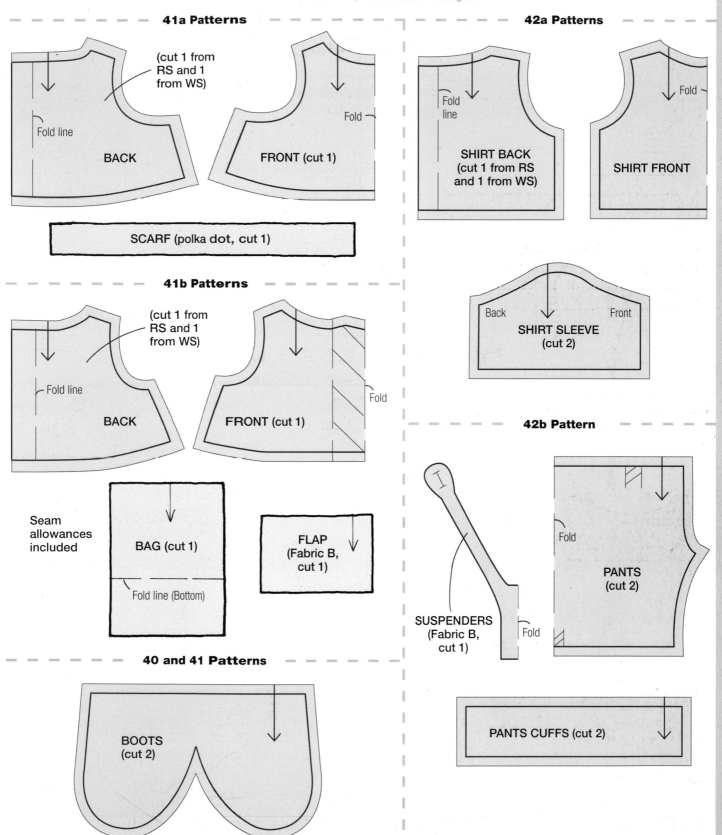

41a Patterns

(cut 1 from RS and 1 from WS)

Fold line

BACK

Fold

FRONT (cut 1)

SCARF (polka dot, cut 1)

41b Patterns

(cut 1 from RS and 1 from WS)

Fold line

BACK

FRONT (cut 1)

Fold

Seam allowances included

BAG (cut 1)

Fold line (Bottom)

FLAP
(Fabric B, cut 1)

42a Patterns

Fold line

SHIRT BACK
(cut 1 from RS and 1 from WS)

Fold

SHIRT FRONT

Back   Front

SHIRT SLEEVE
(cut 2)

42b Pattern

SUSPENDERS
(Fabric B, cut 1)

Fold

Fold

PANTS
(cut 2)

40 and 41 Patterns

BOOTS
(cut 2)

PANTS CUFFS (cut 2)

Patterns for 42 a,b Nick, page 29

Bold line is seam line, outside line is cutting line

42b Patterns

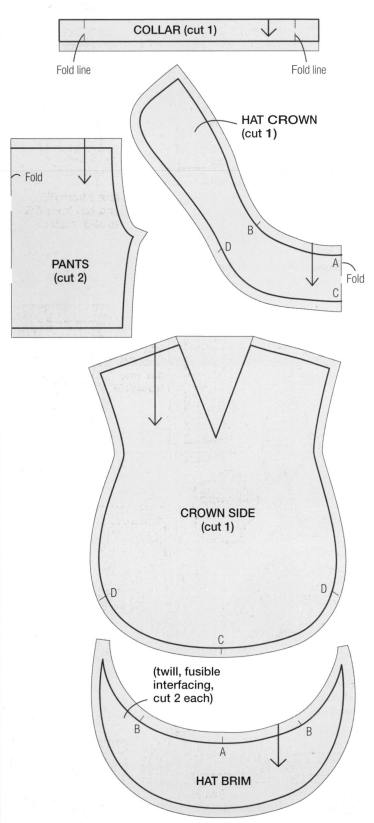

COLLAR (cut 1)

Fold line   Fold line

HAT CROWN
(cut 1)

Fold

B

D

A

Fold

C

PANTS
(cut 2)

CROWN SIDE
(cut 1)

D   D

C

(twill, fusible
interfacing,
cut 2 each)

B   B

A

HAT BRIM

Patterns for 43–45, Cutie body, page 30

Bold line is seam line, outside line is cutting line

NOTE: Mirror images of some pattern pieces are needed for the right and left sides of the doll, so cut pattern on both the fabric's right side and its wrong side.

(cut 2 from WS and two from RS

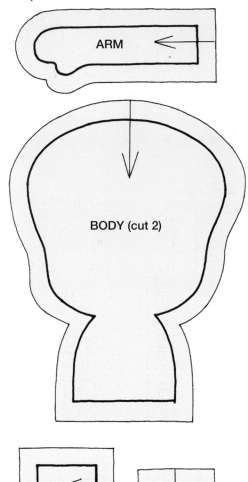

ARM

BODY (cut 2)

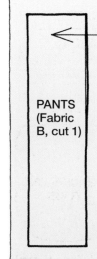

PANTS
(Fabric
B, cut 1)

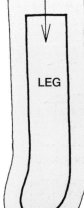

LEG

(cut 2
from WS
and 2
from RS)

Patterns for 43–45, Cutie Pie Dresses up Garments, page 31

Bold line is seam line, outside line is cutting line

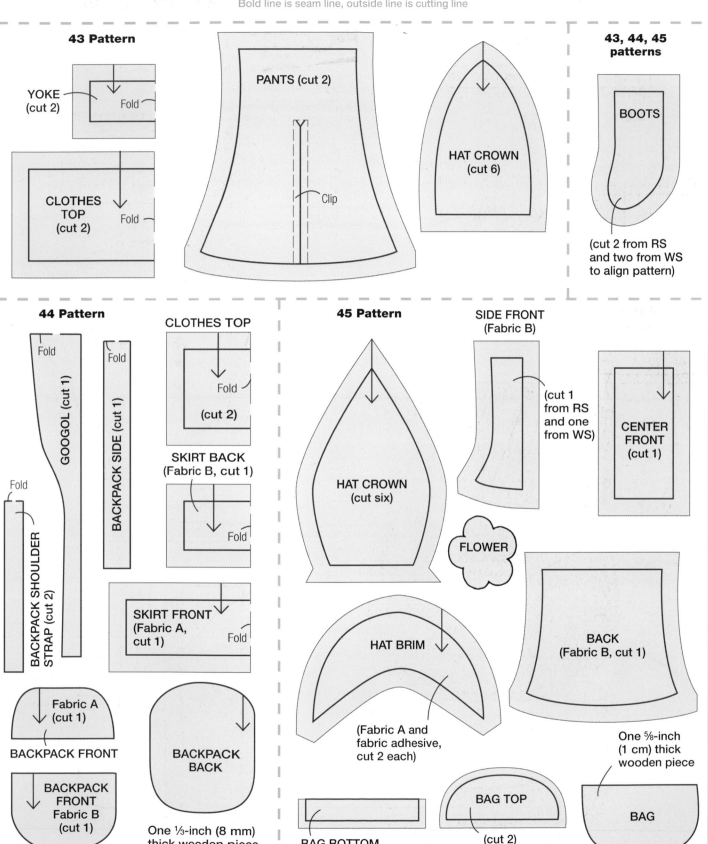

43 Pattern

YOKE (cut 2)
Fold

CLOTHES TOP (cut 2)
Fold

PANTS (cut 2)
Clip

HAT CROWN (cut 6)

43, 44, 45 patterns

BOOTS

(cut 2 from RS and two from WS to align pattern)

44 Pattern

Fold
Fold
GOOGOL (cut 1)
BACKPACK SIDE (cut 1)

Fold
BACKPACK SHOULDER STRAP (cut 2)

CLOTHES TOP
Fold
(cut 2)

SKIRT BACK (Fabric B, cut 1)
Fold

SKIRT FRONT (Fabric A, cut 1)
Fold

Fabric A (cut 1)
BACKPACK FRONT

BACKPACK FRONT Fabric B (cut 1)

BACKPACK BACK

One ⅓-inch (8 mm) thick wooden piece (Fabric A, cut 1)

45 Pattern

HAT CROWN (cut six)

SIDE FRONT (Fabric B)

(cut 1 from RS and one from WS)

CENTER FRONT (cut 1)

FLOWER

HAT BRIM

(Fabric A and fabric adhesive, cut 2 each)

BACK (Fabric B, cut 1)

One ⅝-inch (1 cm) thick wooden piece

BAG

BAG BOTTOM (Fabric B, cut 2)

BAG TOP
(cut 2)

Patterns for 46 Pippi, page 32

Bold line is seam line, outer line is cutting line

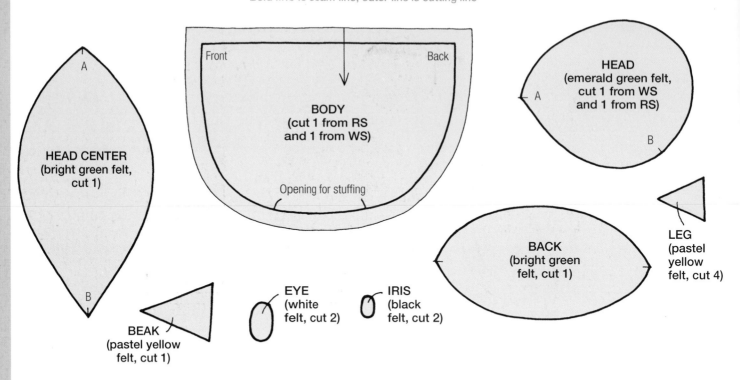

HEAD CENTER
(bright green felt,
cut 1)

A

B

Front

BODY
(cut 1 from RS
and 1 from WS)

Back

Opening for stuffing

HEAD
(emerald green felt,
cut 1 from WS
and 1 from RS)

A

B

LEG
(pastel
yellow
felt, cut 4)

BACK
(bright green
felt, cut 1)

BEAK
(pastel yellow
felt, cut 1)

EYE
(white
felt, cut 2)

IRIS
(black
felt, cut 2)

Patterns for 47 Lilly, page 33

Bold line is seam line, outer line is cutting line

Ear location

Ear location

HEAD Front (cut 1)

LEG (cut 4)

ARM (cut 4)

(Fabric A, B, cut 1 from
RS and 1 from WS)

EAR

In

Out

A

BOTTOM (cut 1)

B

HEAD BACK
(cut 1 from RS
and 1 from WS)

Opening
for
stuffing

BODY
(cut 1 from RS
and 1 from WS)

A

Tail
location

B

Patterns for 48 Dandie, page 32

Bold line is seam line, outer line is cutting line

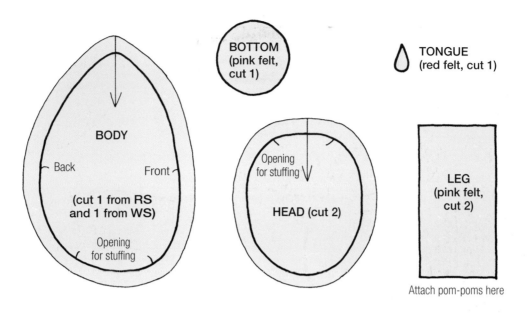

BOTTOM
(pink felt,
cut 1)

TONGUE
(red felt, cut 1)

BODY

Back   Front

(cut 1 from RS
and 1 from WS)

Opening
for stuffing

Opening
for stuffing

HEAD (cut 2)

LEG
(pink felt,
cut 2)

Attach pom-poms here

Patterns for 49–51 Baby Bear Triplets, page 34

Bold line is seam line, outside line is cutting line

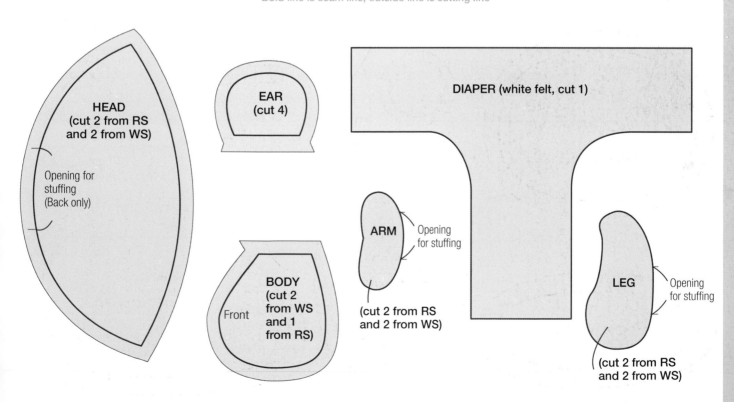

HEAD
(cut 2 from RS
and 2 from WS)

Opening for
stuffing
(Back only)

EAR
(cut 4)

DIAPER (white felt, cut 1)

ARM   Opening
for stuffing

BODY
(cut 2
from WS
and 1
from RS)

Front

(cut 2 from RS
and 2 from WS)

LEG   Opening
for stuffing

(cut 2 from RS
and 2 from WS)

Patterns for 52 He Goat and 53 She Goat Pattern, page 35

page 35

Bold line is seam line, outer line is cutting line

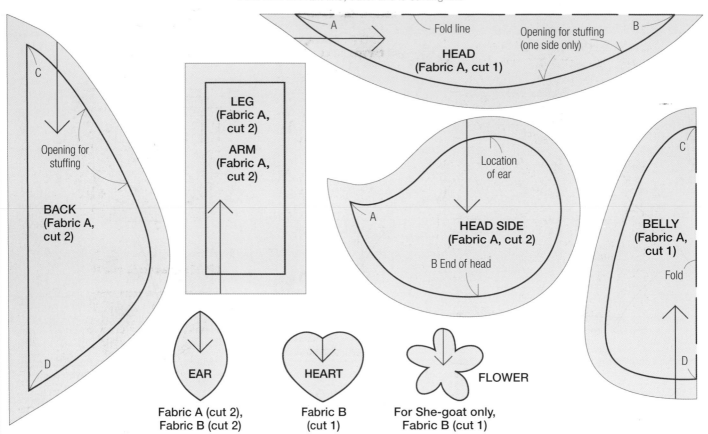

HEAD
(Fabric A, cut 1)

A

Fold line

Opening for stuffing
(one side only)

B

C

Opening for stuffing

BACK
(Fabric A, cut 2)

D

LEG
(Fabric A, cut 2)

ARM
(Fabric A, cut 2)

Location of ear

A

HEAD SIDE
(Fabric A, cut 2)

B End of head

C

BELLY
(Fabric A, cut 1)

Fold

D

EAR
Fabric A (cut 2),
Fabric B (cut 2)

HEART
Fabric B
(cut 1)

FLOWER
For She-goat only,
Fabric B (cut 1)

Pattern for 54 Prairie Bunny and 55 Good Night Bear, pages 36–37

pages 36–37

Bold line is seam line, outer line is cutting line.

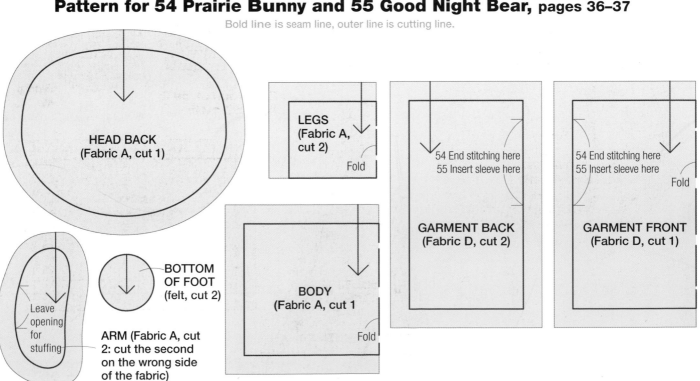

HEAD BACK
(Fabric A, cut 1)

LEGS
(Fabric A, cut 2)

Fold

54 End stitching here
55 Insert sleeve here

GARMENT BACK
(Fabric D, cut 2)

54 End stitching here
55 Insert sleeve here

Fold

GARMENT FRONT
(Fabric D, cut 1)

BOTTOM OF FOOT
(felt, cut 2)

Leave opening for stuffing

BODY
(Fabric A, cut 1

Fold

ARM (Fabric A, cut 2: cut the second on the wrong side of the fabric)

Pattern for 54 Prairie Bunny and 55 Good Night Bear, pages 36–37

Bold line is seam line, outer line is cutting line.

Pattern for Bunny

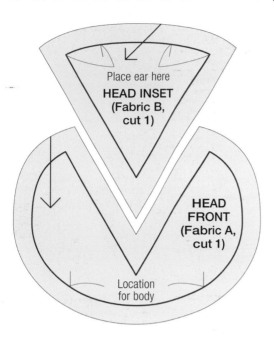

HEAD INSET (Fabric B, cut 1)

Place ear here

HEAD FRONT (Fabric A, cut 1)

Location for body

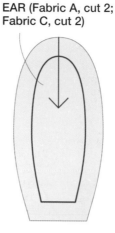

EAR (Fabric A, cut 2; Fabric C, cut 2)

BAG (Fabric F, cut 2)

Back-stitch with 1 strand of red floss

APPLIQUÉ (fabric G, cut 1)

APRON (Fabric E, cut 1)

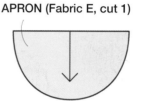

Pattern for Bear

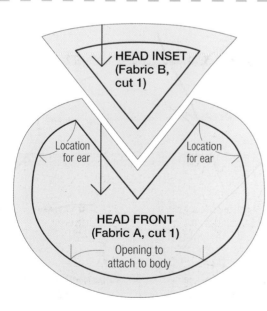

HEAD INSET (Fabric B, cut 1)

Location for ear

Location for ear

HEAD FRONT (Fabric A, cut 1)

Opening to attach to body

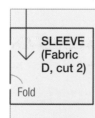

SLEEVE (Fabric D, cut 2)

Fold

EAR (Fabric A, cut 2; Fabric C, cut 2)

NOSE (Fabric C, cut 1)

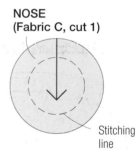

Stitching line

NIGHTCAP (Fabric D, cut 2)

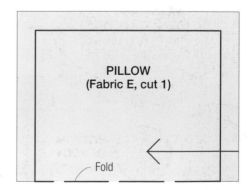

PILLOW (Fabric E, cut 1)

Fold

COME BACK SOON